Auto Repair for Beginners:

The Complete Guide to Solving Your Car's Common Problems on Your Own to Save Money | Uncover DIY Secrets for Your Vehicle with the Insights of a 20-Year Expert Mechanic

Alan Shepard

Table of Contents

Introduction

Have you ever found yourself stranded on the side of the road with a smoking engine and a sinking feeling of helplessness? Or perhaps you've felt the annoyance of shelling out your hard-earned cash on pricey auto repairs only to have the problem recur a few months later. These are the situations that try our patience and deplete our bank accounts. But do not worry; there is a fix for your car problems.

The "Auto Repair & Maintenance: Your Ultimate Guide to Keeping Your Vehicle Running Smoothly" website is pleased to welcome you. We hope that this book will serve as your dependable travel companion as you pursue automotive wisdom. This book is written with you in mind, whether you are an experienced auto enthusiast or a complete novice when it comes to comprehending the inner workings of your vehicle.

Imagine living in a society where you have the knowledge and abilities to identify and repair common auto issues on your own. No more paying for expensive mechanic visits or depending on others to help you with automotive problems. With "Auto Repair & Maintenance," you can learn the inner workings of your car and take charge of its health.

You will go on a journey within these pages that will provide you with the knowledge and skills to handle a variety of vehicle issues. We can help you with everything from straightforward operations like changing a flat tire and performing routine maintenance to more involved repairs like analyzing electrical issues and replacing significant components.

But why should you entrust us to be your navigators on your road trip? I'd like to say hello. I am [Author's Name], a seasoned mechanic with more than 20 years of practical expertise in the auto repair sector. I have dealt with every conceivable automotive issue during my career and have committed myself to locating workable fixes.

I am aware of the hassles and difficulties involved in owning a car. I wrote this book in order to impart my knowledge and experience with you so that you can confidently and easily traverse the world of auto repair and maintenance. You will receive knowledge that can only come from a seasoned professional as you turn each page and take advantage of my years of experience.

"Auto Repair & Maintenance" is not your typical instruction manual. It is especially designed to deal with the issues and pain points that car owners like you frequently experience. This book will provide you the knowledge and abilities you need, whether your goal is to reduce the cost of repairs, increase the lifespan of your automobile, or simply become more independent when it comes to car maintenance.

So, if you're ready to take charge of your automotive future and you're sick of feeling powerless while dealing with car problems, look no further. You should read this book. Prepare to set out on a transforming adventure that will strengthen your position as a car owner and give you the knowledge and assurance to handle any challenges the industry may throw your way.

Now, let's dive into the world of auto repair and maintenance together, and unlock the keys to a smoother, more enjoyable driving experience.

Chapter 1:

Know Your Vehicle

The better equipped you are to maintain and drive your car safely, the more familiar you are with it. The information in this chapter will assist you in understanding the fundamentals of your car as well as the importance of learning about cars and a brief overview of their history. It is intended to assist you in developing an intuitive awareness of your car, beginning with being acquainted with its essential components.

The Essential Components

Owner's Manual

The owner's manual is like the encyclopedia for your car. It includes every bit of information about your car, such as the placement of crucial features like the engine oil dipstick, explanations of the lights and gauges, controls near the steering wheel, pre- and post-trip routines, vehicle maintenance advice, and handling instructions. Anytime you have questions about something in your car, you can consult it.

Vehicle's External and Internal Features

You can operate your car more effectively and easily if you are aware of both its internal and outward aspects. The controls, dials, switches, levers, lights, and symbols found within the car are among these features.

Underneath the Hood

Understanding what's inside the car is just as crucial. This involves being knowledgeable about the transmission system, battery, brake fluid, and coolant. Knowing these parts inside and out might help with routine maintenance and typical auto problems.

Instrument Panel and Steering Column Controls

Controls on the steering wheel and instrument panels are essential for using a car. Although they are made to be intuitive, modern cars nonetheless take some understanding.

Benefits of Vehicle Knowledge

The knowledge of cars offers several distinct benefits:

1. Understanding car values might help you negotiate better prices when purchasing or selling automobiles.
2. Repairing Things Yourself: Regular maintenance, such as changing the oil and rotating the tires, can save you a lot of money.
3. Understanding Repair Costs: You may have more negotiating power if you are aware of the general cost of auto maintenance.
4. Driving Safer Being aware of how brakes and other parts wear down can help you drive more safely.
5. Putting Your Curiosity to Rest: You can have a greater understanding of how cars work.

Brief History of Automobiles

Nicolas-Joseph Cugnot of France created the first real vehicle in 1769, which was propelled by steam. The Duryea brothers created the first successful gasoline-powered automobile in the United States in 1893. Electric motors were easy to operate but ran poorly at high speeds, so manufacturers eventually created cars using them. Due to the higher reliability of gasoline engines and Henry Ford's invention of the assembly line in 1913, mass manufacture of automobiles became feasible.

You'll be better equipped to drive and maintain your own car if you comprehend the mechanics and history of vehicles. The more you understand, the more prepared you'll be to manage anything from basic upkeep to urgent repairs, and the more you'll be able to appreciate the amazing engineering that goes into every vehicle.

The Basics of Vehicle Anatomy

In its most basic form, a vehicle can be thought of as a collection of interconnected systems, each serving a distinct purpose and collaborating to offer movement. It is imperative that we become familiar with these fundamental systems in order to comprehend the fundamentals of vehicle anatomy.

Chassis and Body

The underpart of a vehicle, the chassis, is where the body is mounted. In essence, it offers structural stability and serves as the foundation for mounting numerous vehicular systems. There are two primary chassis types:

- **Body-on-frame chassis**: The vehicle's body rests on top of the frame in this classic type of chassis, and the frame and body have independent functions. Due to its toughness and simplicity of repair, this kind is primarily utilized in trucks and off-road vehicles.
- **Unibody chassis**: In this case, the chassis and body of the vehicle are joined as a single unit and serve as the vehicle's foundation. Modern cars tend to use a unibody frame more frequently since it makes for lighter, more fuel-efficient cars.

Engine and Drivetrain

The engine, which produces the energy needed to propel the car, is its beating heart. On the other hand, the drivetrain consists of the parts of the powertrain other than the engine and transmission. In essence, it transmits engine power to the wheels. Depending on the drive mechanism used, the drivetrain's configuration can change:

- **Front-Wheel Drive (FWD)**: The rear wheels can freely rotate since the power from the engine is transferred through a transaxle and an axle shaft to the front wheels.
- **Rear-Wheel Drive (RWD)**: A driveshaft that spins quickly transfers engine power to a differential that drives the rear wheels.
- **Four-Wheel (4WD)**: All four wheels of the vehicle receive power from the engine. Driveshafts share this engine power between the front and back axles once it has been delivered from the engine to the transmission.
- **All-Wheel Drive (AWD)**: This drivetrain uses a center, rear, and front differential to continuously send power to all four wheels of a vehicle.

Suspension and Steering

By absorbing shocks from irregularities in the road and keeping the tires in contact with the ground, the suspension system contributes to an increase in ride comfort. It is made up of numerous parts that join the car to its wheels, including springs, shock absorbers, and linkages.

On the other side, the steering system is the device that enables the driver to control and steer the car. It consists of items like the steering wheel, steering column, and other connecting pieces that convert the rotation of the steering wheel into wheel rotation.

Brakes and Tires

For a car to be safe, its braking system is essential. It turns the car's kinetic energy into heat energy, allowing the driver to slow down or stop the vehicle. Disc brakes and drum brakes are the two main categories of braking systems, each having specific benefits and uses.

Although frequently overlooked, tires play a crucial role in a vehicle's structure. They play a critical role in vehicle performance and safety because they are the only point of contact between the vehicle and the road surface.

Electrical System

A vehicle's electrical system is made up of a network of parts that produce, store, and transmit electricity. It consists of the starter motor, alternator, battery, and wiring system. The electrical components of your car are powered by this system. A car's electrical system is similar to the circulatory system in the human body. In this comparison, the battery serves as the heart, pumping blood-like electrical current through wires to other car parts. Electrical current flows through the metal body of the car in a single direction, like blood, from the battery to the portion it is powering and then back to the battery.

1. Sub-Systems of the Electrical System

The overall electrical system of the vehicle includes a number of smaller sub-electrical systems, such as:

- **Charging System:** Whilst the car is operating, the electrical system is powered and the battery is kept charged.
- **Ignition System:** Powers the ignition and combustion process.
- **Starting System:** Powers the starter motor to start the vehicle's engine.
- **Fuel System:** Monitors and manages the fuel consumption.

2. Major Components

The fuse, relay, battery, alternator, and starting motor are the main elements of an automobile's electrical system.

- **Battery:** The vehicle's battery stores electricity produced by the alternator and sends it to the supplementary circuits, which power the lights. The majority of batteries have a 12 volt rating and have an output range of 200 to 1000 amps.
- **Alternator:** The battery is recharged and the electrical system of the car is powered by the alternator.
- **Starter Motor:** The starter motor starts the engine using electricity.
- **Fuse and Relay:** These safety tools are employed to guard against potential harm from electrical surges or short circuits to the vehicle's electrical systems.

3. Electrical Circuit Types

The electrical system of the car is closed circuit, which means it creates a loop through which the electrical current can move. There are several different kinds of electrical circuits, including parallel, series, open, closed, and short circuits.

4. Electrical Terminologies

Understanding the following phrases can help you better understand how the electrical system in your car operates:

- **Current:** the amount of electricity flowing via a circuit, expressed in amps (amps).
- **Voltage:** the force, expressed in volts, that drives the circuit's current.
- **Resistance:** the amount of current flow a wire resists, expressed in ohms. Compared to thick ones, thin wires have a higher resistance.
- **Watt:** A component's power consumption can be calculated by multiplying the amps and volts.

Knowing how the electrical system works inside the car might help with maintenance and potential problems. Although we have gone over the fundamentals, keep in mind that this is a complex system. A professional should always be consulted if in doubt.

Types Of Vehicles

1. **Sedan or Saloon**: One of the most popular car kinds are sedans, commonly referred to as saloons. They are distinguished by a four-door design with a conventional trunk dividing the passenger and freight spaces. These cars easily accommodate five passengers and have a modest amount of baggage capacity. Sedans like the Nissan Altima and Honda Accord make terrific examples.
2. **Estate or Wagon**: The estate, also known as a station wagon, is a vehicle with a longer roofline and a hatch door in place of a trunk in the back. Compared to sedans, this design offers a larger load capacity. Some models, like the Subaru Outback and Audi A4 Allroad, are built to seem like SUVs, complete with high ground clearance and tough body armor.
3. **Sports Cars**: Sports cars are made to function well at high speeds and look good. These vehicles, like the Porsche 911 and Mazda Miata, are frequently

pricey, elegant, and low to the ground. Although some models include tiny back seats, they typically only have two seats.

4. **Pickup Trucks**: Pickup trucks are practical vehicles with an exposed bed or cargo area behind the passenger compartment. They are frequently utilized for off-road situations or while transporting large objects. Depending on the size of the cab, they have seating for two to five persons.

5. **Hatchbacks**: Compact cars called "hatchbacks" have a rear flip-up hatch door that allows access to the trunk. They are typically more spacious than a regular trunk and have a squared-off roof. The Kia Rio and Volkswagen Golf are two examples.

6. **Sport Utility Vehicles (SUVs)**: SUVs have a higher seating position and more ground clearance than sedans since they are taller and boxier. They frequently include a cargo space that resembles a station wagon and have three rows of seats that may accommodate five to seven passengers. Off-road capabilities are frequently found in SUVs, which also feature cutting-edge electronics for comfort and convenience.

7. **Family Vans or Minivans**: Family vans, often known as minivans, are vehicles made mainly for carrying large groups of people, including families. They provide roomy interiors with adaptable seating configurations, frequently for seven or more passengers. In minivans, comfort, safety, and convenience features frequently take precedence over performance. Minivans like the Chrysler Pacifica and Honda Odyssey are excellent examples.

8. **Buses**: Buses are substantial automobiles that are mostly utilized for public transportation. They are frequently utilized in both urban and intercity transit systems and have a huge passenger capacity. Depending on their specialized usage, they come in a variety of sizes and shapes, from small school buses to double-decker and articulated buses.

Chapter 2:

The Crucial Role of Regular Car Maintenance

Maintaining your car's functioning, performance, and longevity is crucially dependent on routine maintenance. In addition to saving you money on expensive repair costs, putting a strong emphasis on preventive measures greatly improves the safety of your driving journey.

Why Ignoring Regular Maintenance is a Costly Mistake

Ignoring routine auto maintenance is similar to putting one's finances and safety at danger by digging a deep pit. In the case of car maintenance, the adage "if it ain't broke, don't fix it" does not hold true. In fact, the consequences of neglect can be severe, with costs for repairs, car breakdowns, and even traffic accidents as a result of defective parts.

The term "preventive maintenance" refers to a sequence of regular and routine servicing procedures intended to stop unanticipated equipment faults. It all comes down to foreseeing potential problems in advance, reducing risks, and handling small difficulties as soon as they emerge to prevent larger ones from developing. Neglecting routine maintenance could result in catastrophic problems that would cost far more than what would have been incurred by routine examinations and small repairs.

For instance, if a small problem with your brake system is discovered early enough, it may be inexpensive and straightforward to correct. However, ignoring this could result in a complete brake system failure, a risk that puts both you and other road users in danger. This risk may have been reduced with a quick preventive maintenance procedure like checking the quality of your brake pads or brake fluid levels.

Boosting Your Vehicle's Performance and Lifespan with Regular Maintenance

Regular auto maintenance also improves performance and increases the lifespan of your car in addition to preventing problems. You can keep your car running at its best by routinely monitoring the fluid levels, repairing worn-out parts, and taking care of minor concerns. This not only results in a better driving experience, but it also lengthens the useful life of your car.

For instance, keeping your engine clean and well-lubricated requires replacing the oil at the manufacturer's suggested intervals. By doing so, friction is lessened, which helps the engine run more efficiently and prevents unnecessary wear and tear on its parts.

Improving Safety on the Road: The Underestimated Power of Preventive Care

The considerable contribution that car maintenance makes to road safety is one element that is sometimes overlooked. Your car's brakes, lighting, tires, and every other part all contribute to making the trip safe. Regular inspections and maintenance procedures ensure that these parts work as they should.

For instance, maintaining good tire condition by making sure they are filled properly and have enough tread can greatly lower the danger of a blowout and provide a safer ride. The stopping power and visibility of your car are improved by promptly replacing worn-out brake pads and windshield wipers, respectively. This increases safety.

In conclusion, routine preventative maintenance for cars is an essential aspect of automotive ownership. In addition to enhancing vehicle performance and protecting your investment, it also helps to assure your safety while driving. Always follow the manufacturer's instructions listed in your vehicle's owner's manual to stay on top of your maintenance schedule, and think about utilizing a maintenance calendar to keep track of these important duties.

Understanding the Different Components of Your Car and Their Maintenance Needs

The longevity and safety of the vehicle depend on routine maintenance. Here, we examine several auto parts and their upkeep requirements, highlighting the significance of frequent inspections and preventative measures.

The Vital Importance of Engine Maintenance: Beyond the Oil Change

The engine, a sophisticated system of interrelated pieces that powers your car, is at the center of your car. Spark plugs, drive belts, timing belts or chains, air and fluid filters, and other crucial components all contribute to keeping your engine in peak working order. It's essential to maintain these parts on a regular basis to spot potential issues early and guarantee your car runs as smoothly as possible.

You should check the oil and coolant levels in your engine once a month, or every few gas fill-ups, when the engine is cool. If any or both are present in low quantities, they have the potential to cause serious engine issues.

Brake Pads and Windshield Wipers: The Unsung Heroes of Road Safety

Your car's brake pads and windshield wipers are important safety features that are frequently neglected. To make sure they work properly, these parts should be frequently inspected and changed when necessary. Your safety while driving can be jeopardized by brake pads or windshield wipers that aren't properly maintained, especially in bad weather.

The Intricacies of Automobile Engines and Their Maintenance Requirements

Automobile engines are complex systems that need close scrutiny. To avoid future costly repairs, you must understand the particular requirements of your engine. Inspections on a regular basis can identify potential problems before they develop into larger ones.

The air filter in your engine controls air flow into the engine and filters out trash and particles. Making sure your air filter is working properly can increase fuel economy, lower pollutants, and lengthen the life of your engine.

The Role of Fluids in Your Vehicle's Health: More than Just Fuel and Oil

Fluids are essential to the functionality and health of your car. Other fluids, including as brake and power steering fluids, as well as radiator coolant, are as important in addition to oil and coolant. As part of preventive maintenance, regular checks of these fluid levels guarantee the efficient operation of your car.

Overviews of the various parts of your car and their upkeep needs are provided in this chapter. In later chapters, we'll go into more detail about the major components' individual maintenance requirements.

To ensure a safe and effective ride, keep in mind that proactive maintenance and early detection of any faults can help you avoid expensive repairs down the road. For detailed maintenance schedules and instructions, always consult your vehicle's owner's manual as these may vary between different makes and models.

Scheduled Maintenance Check-Ups

When it comes to car maintenance, the adage "An ounce of prevention is worth a pound of cure" remains true. Maintaining a regular maintenance schedule is essential for car owners, not only to keep the car running smoothly and efficiently, but also to prevent future, potentially expensive repairs. The car maintenance schedule involves monthly, quarterly, biannual, yearly, and six-monthly inspections, each with a specific focus.

Monthly, 3-Month, and 6-Month Check-ups

Monthly Check-ups: Monthly check-ups are the first step in your vehicle's routine checkup. They are essential in identifying the beginning of prospective problems so you may address them before they worsen. The focus of monthly inspections is on checking the amount of oil and coolant, the state of the air filters, and the tire pressure and tread depth. It's also crucial to frequently check the operation of your headlights, turn signals, brake, and parking lights.

3-Month Check-ups: The range of examinations expands as the time between them does. In addition to the regular monthly checks, your car should get a thorough inspection of its belts, hoses, and brakes every three months. These parts are essential to the safe and effective running of your car, and taking care of minor wear and tear now can stop more serious problems later.

6-Month Check-ups: The more thorough six-month inspections include checks for engine oil changes and a careful examination of the fuel and air filters. Depending on the make and type of your vehicle, you might now need to swap out the spark plugs.

Annual and Biennial Check-ups

Annual Check-ups: Annual maintenance inspections concentrate on the car's general appearance and functionality, including evaluations of the steering and suspension systems. This thorough evaluation makes sure that your car will run at its best for the upcoming year.

Biennial Check-ups: Your car needs a thorough examination every two years that includes checking the timing belts or chains and replacing the fluid and air filters. If these long-term components are ignored, it may result in serious problems and expensive repairs.

Long-Term Check-ups: Ensuring Your Vehicle's Health for Years to Come

Long-term inspections concentrate on the durability and general health of your car. These evaluations often entail the replacement of high-wear components as well as a careful inspection of all the vehicle's systems. They are essential to preserving your car's value and ensuring its continued operation.

The goal of the preventive approach to automotive maintenance is to deal with minor faults before they develop into larger ones. This will ensure the longevity of your vehicle. As particular schedules and requirements may differ, always refer to your vehicle's owner's manual for the manufacturer's recommended maintenance regimen. You may have a smooth and worry-free driving experience by adhering to a well-organized and disciplined maintenance schedule.

Since the 1930s, car warranties have advanced significantly, with current coverage lengths ranging from three to five years, up from just three months in the past. Because a large portion of a vehicle's useful life now falls inside the warranty term, preventive maintenance is more crucial than ever for lowering the risk of failures brought on by deterioration over time.

Why Ignoring Maintenance Guidelines Might Void Your Warranty

Ignoring the advised maintenance recommendations may cause a product to fail early or late owing to manufacture flaws or degradation, respectively. Most of the time, if these problems happen as a result of disregarding the recommended preventative maintenance program, a warranty will not cover them. Therefore, skipping preventive maintenance puts your warranty at risk in addition to increasing the likelihood that your car may age more quickly.

The Importance of Detailed Service Records in Keeping Your Warranty Valid

Maintaining thorough service records is essential to maintaining the validity of your warranty, especially when it comes to preventive maintenance. These documents serve as evidence that you followed the manufacturer's maintenance instructions when servicing the car. The date, information on the maintenance that was carried out, and the distance at the time of service should all be included in the service records.

Investing in Your Car's Future through Preventive Maintenance

Preventive maintenance expenditures made during the warranty period can significantly reduce the owner's post-warranty maintenance costs. Usage-based, calendar/time-based, predictive, and prescriptive maintenance are some examples of preventive maintenance techniques. You effectively revitalize your vehicle by doing routine inspections, lubrications, and replacements when necessary, so extending its useful life and ensuring it continues to be fully functional.

How Regular Maintenance Helps You Save Money in the Long Run

Even though it may seem like an unnecessary investment in the near term, routine preventative maintenance can help you save money in the long run. Preventive maintenance assists in locating and resolving minor issues before they become more serious and expensive concerns. Additionally, it boosts the performance of your car, increases fuel economy, and lowers the possibility of problems, saving you money on gasoline and potential repair expenses.

Turning Maintenance into a Routine

Making preventive maintenance a habit is crucial for a vehicle's longevity and health. Regular inspections and small repairs like oil changes, tire rotations, and brake inspections are included in routine maintenance. Making this a regular guarantees your automobile stays in top shape and lowers the likelihood of unplanned breakdowns or pricey repairs in the future.

It is essential to keep in mind that preventive maintenance is essential if you want to make the most of the benefits of your car's warranty. It not only maintains the validity of your warranty but also lowers your long-term costs and guarantees that your car will run efficiently and dependably for its entire lifespan.

Chapter 3:

Engine Repair

Engines are the heart of any vehicle or machinery, providing the necessary power to propel them forward. Like any complex system, engines require regular maintenance and repair to ensure optimal performance and longevity. Engine repair encompasses a wide range of tasks aimed at diagnosing and addressing issues related to various engine components. By understanding the intricacies of engine control, ignition, fuel systems, and emission control, it becomes possible to effectively troubleshoot and fix problems that may arise. In this article, we will delve into the key aspects of engine repair, exploring the vital components and systems that contribute to a smooth and efficient operation.

The engine is the heart of a car, responsible for converting heat from burning fuel into the force that propels the vehicle. Over the years, engines have evolved from mechanical, pneumatic, or hydraulic systems to electronic control systems. This chapter will provide a comprehensive understanding of automotive engines, including their components, working principles, and various engine layouts.

Components of an Engine

An automotive engine consists of several key components that work together to generate power. The two main parts are the cylinder block and the cylinder head. The cylinder block houses the crankshaft, which converts the reciprocating motion of the pistons into rotary motion. It also contains the camshaft, responsible for operating the valves in the cylinder head. The cylinder head, on the other hand, contains passages for air and fuel mixture intake and exhaust gas expulsion.

Working Principles

The engine operates on the principle of internal combustion, where a spark ignites a mixture of petrol vapor and compressed air inside a sealed cylinder. This ignition causes the mixture to burn rapidly, producing expanding gases that provide power to drive the car. The crankshaft converts the reciprocating motion of the pistons into rotary motion, which ultimately turns the road wheels.

Engine Layouts

There are several engine layouts commonly used in automotive design:

1. **In-line Engine:** This layout consists of four or more cylinders arranged vertically in a row. It is the simplest and most common type of engine, with larger capacities often having six cylinders in line [2].
2. **V-Engine:** The V-engine layout is more compact and is often used in vehicles with eight, twelve, or six cylinders. The cylinders are arranged opposite each other at an angle, typically up to 90 degrees [2].
3. **Horizontally-Opposed Engine**: This layout is an extension of the V-engine layout, with the cylinder angle widened to 180 degrees. It offers advantages in terms of space-saving and balance [2].

Electronic Engine Control

The advent of electronic control systems revolutionized engine control in the automotive industry. Electronic engine control involves regulating fuel and air intake, as well as spark timing, to achieve the desired performance in terms of torque or power output. It replaced older mechanical, pneumatic, and hydraulic systems that were used before the 1970s. The electronic control systems provide more precise control and better adaptability to various driving conditions.

Understanding automotive engines is essential for anyone interested in cars, whether as a technician, student, or enthusiast. This chapter provided an overview of the components of an engine, their working principles, and various engine layouts. It also highlighted the significance of electronic engine control in achieving optimal performance. A solid grasp of these concepts will contribute to a comprehensive understanding of automotive engines and their operation.

Engine Components and Systems

We will covers essential components and systems that contribute to the overall operation of an internal combustion engine. Let's examine the key components mentioned in the provided information:

1. **Cylinder Block:** The cylinder block is a critical component of an internal combustion engine. It serves as the main structure that houses the engine's cylinders and provides support for other components. The cylinder block is designed to withstand high temperatures and pressures generated during the combustion process. It is typically made of cast iron or cast steel and plays a crucial role in facilitating processes such as intake, compression, combustion, and exhaust within the engine.
2. **Cylinder Head:** The cylinder head is located at the top of the engine cylinder and acts as a cover. It seals the combustion chamber, preventing the entry and exit of air and gases. In a petrol engine, it houses components like the spark plug, inlet and exhaust valves, and fuel injectors in a diesel engine. Cylinder heads are usually made of cast iron or aluminum and are essential for maintaining the integrity of the combustion chamber.
3. **Piston**: The piston is a crucial moving component within the engine cylinder. It undergoes reciprocating motion as a result of the combustion process. The piston transfers mechanical energy to the crankshaft through the connecting rod. Pistons are designed to be strong and lightweight, capable of withstanding high pressures and temperatures. They are commonly made of cast iron or aluminum alloy.
4. **Piston Rings:** Piston rings provide a sealing effect between the piston and the cylinder wall. They ensure that the combustion gases do not leak past the piston

and allow for efficient energy transfer. Piston rings are crucial for maintaining compression within the engine cylinder. By preventing gas leakage, they contribute to the overall performance and efficiency of the engine.

These are just a few examples of the engine components covered in the chapter. Other components mentioned include connecting rods, crankshafts, combustion chambers, manifolds, valves, spark plugs, fuel injectors, and many more. Each component plays a specific role in the engine's operation and contributes to its overall performance and efficiency.

Understanding the intricacies of engine components and systems is vital for engineers and enthusiasts alike. By studying and comprehending these components, engineers can optimize engine design and performance, leading to more efficient and reliable engines.

Engine Operation Principles

An internal combustion engine (ICE) is a type of heat engine that operates based on the principles of combustion and energy conversion. It is widely used in various applications, including cars, aircraft, boats, and power generation. The engine utilizes the combustion of fuel and oxidizer, usually air, to generate high-temperature and high-pressure gases, which then exert force on engine components to produce mechanical work. Let's explore the principles of engine operation in more detail.

1. **Combustion Process:** The internal combustion process is the fundamental principle behind the operation of an engine. It involves the controlled combustion of a fuel-air mixture within the engine's combustion chamber. The most common fuels used in ICEs are hydrocarbon-based, such as gasoline, diesel fuel, natural gas, ethanol, or biodiesel. The combustion process consists of the following stages:

Intake: The fuel-air mixture is drawn into the combustion chamber during the intake stroke as the piston moves downward. In spark ignition engines (gasoline engines), the fuel is mixed with air prior to entering the chamber. In compression ignition engines (diesel engines), only air is drawn into the chamber during this stage.

Compression: The piston moves upward during the compression stroke, compressing the fuel-air mixture or just the air in the combustion chamber. This compression raises the temperature and pressure inside the chamber.

Combustion and Power Stroke: In spark ignition engines, a spark plug ignites the compressed fuel-air mixture, initiating combustion. The ignited mixture rapidly burns, releasing energy in the form of expanding gases. This combustion forces the piston downward, generating mechanical work and torque. In compression ignition engines, fuel is injected into the hot compressed air, causing spontaneous ignition and combustion.

Exhaust: After the power stroke, the exhaust stroke begins as the piston moves upward, expelling the combustion byproducts, including gases, such as carbon dioxide and water vapor, and other pollutants through the exhaust valves.

2. **Conversion of Energy**: The combustion process converts the chemical energy stored in the fuel into thermal energy, which is then converted into mechanical work. The expanding gases from combustion exert pressure on the piston, transferring energy to the connecting rod and crankshaft. The crankshaft converts the linear motion of the piston into rotary motion, which can be used to power various applications, such as turning the wheels of a vehicle or generating electricity.

3. **Types of Internal Combustion Engines:** There are several types of internal combustion engines, each with its specific design and operating characteristics. The two most common types are:

Spark Ignition Engines (Gasoline Engines): These engines use a spark plug to ignite the fuel-air mixture. They operate on a four-stroke cycle, known as the Otto cycle, which includes intake, compression, combustion/power stroke, and exhaust strokes.

Compression Ignition Engines (Diesel Engines): Diesel engines compress only air during the compression stroke. Fuel is injected into the hot, highly compressed air, causing self-ignition and combustion. Diesel engines also operate on a four-stroke cycle but are known as the diesel cycle.

4. **Engine Components:** Key components of an internal combustion engine include:

Cylinder: The cylinder provides a chamber for the combustion process. Pistons move up and down inside the cylinders.

Piston: Pistons are cylindrical components that reciprocate within the cylinders, transferring force from the expanding gases to the crankshaft.

Crankshaft: The crankshaft converts the linear motion of the pistons into rotary motion, which is then used to transmit power.

Valves: Intake and exhaust valves control the flow of fuel-air mixture and exhaust gases into and out of the combustion chamber.

Spark Plug (in gasoline engines): The spark plug generates an electric spark to ignite the fuel-air mixture.

Fuel Injection System (in diesel engines): The fuel injection system injects fuel into the combustion chamber at the appropriate time.

Cooling System: Engines have cooling systems, such as radiators and coolant, to manage and dissipate the heat generated during operation.

5. **Advancements and Efficiency:** Over the years, significant advancements have been made in improving the performance and efficiency of internal combustion engines. Research and development efforts have focused on reducing emissions, increasing fuel economy, and optimizing engine design. These advancements include technologies like direct fuel injection, turbocharging, variable valve timing, hybrid powertrains, and advanced engine management systems.

Engine operation principles revolve around the combustion process, energy conversion, and the interaction of various components within the engine. The combustion of fuel and oxidizer generates high-pressure gases that produce mechanical work, enabling the engine to power different applications. Advancements in engine technology continue to enhance efficiency, reduce emissions, and improve overall performance.

Engine Diagnostics

Engine diagnostics refer to the process of identifying and analyzing issues or faults in an engine system. It involves the use of diagnostic tools, equipment, and procedures to determine the root cause of engine problems and provide accurate diagnoses. By understanding engine diagnostics, technicians and engineers can effectively identify and resolve issues, ensuring optimal engine performance and reliability.

Common Engine Problems and Symptoms:

1. Misfiring: Engine misfiring occurs when one or more cylinders fail to ignite properly. Symptoms include rough idling, loss of power, and a noticeable decrease in fuel efficiency.
2. Overheating: Engine overheating can result from various issues such as coolant leaks, a malfunctioning thermostat, or a faulty radiator. Symptoms include high engine temperature readings, steam coming from the engine, and frequent coolant loss.
3. Poor Acceleration: If an engine experiences a lack of power or struggles to accelerate, it may indicate issues with the fuel system, such as clogged fuel injectors or a failing fuel pump.
4. Excessive Exhaust Smoke: Different colored exhaust smoke can indicate various problems. For example, black smoke may indicate excessive fuel consumption, blue smoke suggests oil burning, and white smoke could indicate coolant entering the combustion chamber.
5. Engine Stalling: Engine stalling can occur due to various reasons, including a faulty ignition system, clogged fuel filters, or a malfunctioning sensor. Symptoms include the engine shutting off unexpectedly while driving or idling.

Diagnostic Tools and Equipment:

1. OBD-II Scanner: An On-Board Diagnostics (OBD-II) scanner is a crucial tool for engine diagnostics. It plugs into the OBD-II port of a vehicle and retrieves diagnostic trouble codes (DTCs) stored in the engine control unit (ECU). These codes provide information about specific issues in the engine system.
2. Multimeter: A multimeter is used to measure electrical voltages, currents, and resistances. It helps diagnose problems related to electrical components, such as sensors, wiring, and ignition systems.

3. Compression Tester: A compression tester is used to measure the compression pressure within each cylinder. Low compression levels can indicate problems with the piston rings, valves, or head gasket.
4. Fuel Pressure Gauge: This tool is used to measure the fuel pressure in the fuel system. It helps diagnose issues related to fuel delivery, such as a failing fuel pump or a clogged fuel filter.
5. Oscilloscope: An oscilloscope is used to analyze electrical signals and waveforms. It can be helpful in diagnosing issues with sensors, ignition systems, and other electrical components.

Diagnostic Procedures and Techniques:

1. Visual Inspection: A visual inspection involves examining the engine components for any visible signs of damage, leaks, or loose connections. This step helps identify obvious issues before proceeding with further diagnostics.
2. Reading Diagnostic Trouble Codes (DTCs): Using an OBD-II scanner, technicians retrieve DTCs stored in the ECU. These codes provide information about specific faults or malfunctions in the engine system, guiding the diagnostic process.
3. Functional Testing: Functional testing involves conducting tests on various engine components and systems to assess their performance. This can include checking sensor readings, fuel pressure, ignition spark, and exhaust emissions.
4. Data Analysis: Analyzing data from sensors, diagnostic tools, and the engine control module helps identify patterns, anomalies, or correlations that can point towards specific engine problems.
5. Component Testing: Testing individual components, such as sensors, ignition coils, or fuel injectors, can help determine if they are functioning correctly. This can be done using specialized testing equipment or by comparing their performance against specifications.

By following these diagnostic procedures and utilizing the appropriate tools and equipment, technicians can accurately identify engine problems, determine the root cause, and take appropriate steps to, 1 messages not shown.

10 Care Tips That Will Keep Your Motor Running Strong

Proper engine maintenance is essential for keeping your motor running smoothly and ensuring its longevity. By following these ten care tips, you can keep your engine in optimal condition and avoid costly repairs in the future.

1. Change the Oil: Regularly changing the engine oil is crucial for maintaining its performance. Engine oil lubricates the moving parts, reduces friction, and helps remove contaminants. Follow the manufacturer's recommendations for oil change intervals and use the appropriate oil grade for your vehicle.

2. Clean the Engine: Keeping your engine clean helps prevent the buildup of dirt, debris, and grime that can affect its performance. Use a gentle degreaser and a soft brush to clean the engine components, taking care to avoid sensitive areas such as electrical connections and sensors.

3. Replace the Air Filter: The air filter ensures that clean air reaches the engine for combustion. Over time, the air filter can become clogged with dirt and debris, reducing airflow and engine efficiency. Replace the air filter regularly, typically every 12 months or 12,000 miles, to maintain optimal engine performance.

4. Use Original Parts: When replacing components in your engine, it's best to use original parts or high-quality aftermarket parts that meet the manufacturer's specifications. Original parts are designed specifically for your engine, ensuring proper fit, function, and durability.

5. Use Clean Fuel: Using clean and high-quality fuel is essential for the optimal performance of your engine. Contaminated fuel can lead to fuel system issues and engine damage. Fill up at reputable gas stations and consider using fuel additives to keep your fuel system clean and protect against deposits.

6. Check the Battery: The battery provides electrical power to start the engine and run various electrical components. Regularly inspect the battery terminals for corrosion and clean them if necessary. Ensure the battery is securely fastened and check its voltage periodically to ensure it's in good condition.

7. Change the Belts: Inspect the engine belts for signs of wear, cracks, or fraying. Over time, belts can deteriorate and lose their tension, affecting the performance of components such as the alternator, power steering pump, and air conditioning. Replace worn-out belts to prevent unexpected failures.

8. Check Fluids: Regularly check the levels and condition of engine fluids, including coolant, brake fluid, power steering fluid, and transmission fluid. Low or contaminated fluids can cause overheating, poor braking performance, and

other issues. Refer to your vehicle's owner's manual for the recommended fluid inspection intervals.

9. Replace Spark Plugs: Spark plugs play a vital role in the combustion process by igniting the air-fuel mixture. Over time, spark plugs can become fouled or worn, leading to misfires, reduced fuel efficiency, and poor engine performance. Replace spark plugs according to the manufacturer's recommendations to ensure optimal combustion.

10. Fix Small Problems: Addressing small issues promptly can prevent them from turning into major engine problems. Regularly inspect your engine for leaks, unusual noises, or warning lights. If you notice anything out of the ordinary, have it checked by a qualified mechanic and address the problem before it worsens.

By following these ten care tips, you can keep your engine in excellent condition, maximize its performance, and extend its lifespan. Remember to consult your vehicle's owner's manual for specific maintenance guidelines and intervals that apply to your make and model. Regular engine maintenance will contribute to a smooth and trouble-free driving experience.

Chapter 4:

Automotive Electrical System Repair

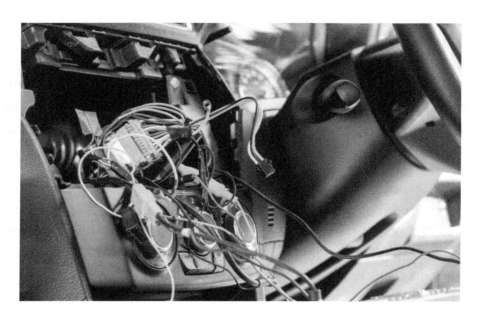

Ensuring a Smooth Ride

The best performance and dependability of automobiles depend on a working electrical system. The electrical system gives the vehicle the power it needs to start the engine, run onboard computers, keep an eye on sensors, and do other tasks. In this blog post, we'll look at the various parts of the automotive electrical system, talk about typical electrical system problems and their symptoms, get into troubleshooting methods, outline how to diagnose and fix electrical issues with cars, give maintenance advice, and discuss when to call a pro. Understanding these elements will enable you to handle electrical problems quickly, resulting in a safer and more pleasurable driving experience.

Understanding the Automotive Electrical System

The automobile electrical system is made up of numerous important parts that work together to supply power and enable different tasks inside the car. You may be able to better understand the system's complexity if you are familiar with these parts.

A. Battery The engine may be started and the electrical parts of the car are powered by the battery, which is the main power source in the electrical system. It stores chemical energy and uses a chemical reaction to transform it into electrical energy, supplying the required voltage to run the vehicle.

B. Alternator When the engine is running, the alternator is essential for powering the electrical system and recharging the battery. In order to maintain a steady supply of power for the vehicle's parts and accessories, it transforms the mechanical energy from the engine's rotation into electrical energy.

C. beginning motor The ignition of the engine's combustion cycle is started by the starter motor. It turns the engine's crankshaft using electrical power from the battery, which causes the pistons to compress the air-fuel combination and light the spark plugs, starting the engine.

D. Spiking plugs Essential parts that ignite the air-fuel mixture in the engine's cylinders are spark plugs. In order to start combustion, they produce an electric spark, which guarantees effective engine operation and power delivery.

E. Wiring devices By linking different electrical components and guaranteeing the seamless transmission of electrical signals throughout the vehicle, wiring harnesses serve as the nervous system of the car. They are made up of a web of wires and connectors that have been thoughtfully designed and routed to produce strong and dependable electrical connections.

Signs of Electrical System Issues

It's essential to recognize typical electrical system faults in order to spot possible concerns and take proper action to fix them. Here are some signs that your car might have an electrical issue underneath:

➢ flashing or dim lighting While the car is operating, you can notice that your dashboard, interior, or headlight lights are fading or flickering. This could be a sign that something is wrong with the electrical system. This can indicate a broken alternator, a weak battery, or shoddy electrical connections.
➢ Having trouble starting the car Starting your car slowly or with difficulty could be a sign of an electrical problem. The causes of the starting issues may be a weak or dead battery, a defective starter motor, or issues with the ignition switch.
➢ faulty electrical components If any of your car's electrical systems, like the power windows, the central locking system, or the infotainment system, start acting strangely or stop working completely, it may be a symptom of an electrical problem. Damaged switches, bad wiring, or problems with control modules could all be to blame for this.
➢ Unusual noises or odors Unusual noises, like clicking or buzzing, or odd odors, like a burning stench, can be signs of electrical system issues. These symptoms could be caused by poor wiring, harmed parts, or an electrical overload.

Troubleshooting Common Car Electrical Problems

When dealing with automotive electrical issues, it's critical to accurately diagnose and resolve them. Here are some typical problems you could experience and how to fix them:

➢ fuse blowouts Specific components may stop functioning as a result of blown fuses obstructing the flow of electrical electricity. Investigate the underlying reason of the fuse blowout, such as a short circuit or an excessive load, before replacing the bad fuse with a new one of the same rating to resolve this issue.
➢ damaged alternator Battery discharge and electrical component failure can occur as a result of an alternator problem. Utilizing a multimeter, start by determining the alternator's output voltage. The output may indicate a defective alternator that needs to be replaced if it falls below the advised range.
➢ Low battery A dead battery may prevent your car from starting or result in sporadic electrical problems. Start by using a multimeter to check the battery voltage. Recharge the battery or replace it if necessary if the voltage falls below the required level. Additionally, look for any corrosion or loose connections on the battery connectors that can impair its correct operation.

- defective starter motor A defective starter motor may be the cause of delayed or nonexistent cranking when your car starts. Make that the connections between the starter motor and the battery are clean and secure. If the connections are sound but the starter motor still has problems, it could need to be replaced.
- faulty spark plugs Spark plugs that are worn out or broken can cause misfires, poor engine performance, and trouble starting the car. Check the spark plugs for wear indicators like eroded electrodes or carbon buildup. To keep your engine running at its best, replace any spark plugs that are damaged in accordance with the manufacturer's instructions.
- Incorrect ignition switch A defective ignition switch may result in sporadic starting problems or a complete inability to start. Turning the key and watching what happens will test the ignition switch. It could be necessary to have the switch replaced by a skilled automobile technician if it is nonresponsive or exhibiting failure symptoms.
- unreliable power window motor A issue with the power window motor may be the cause of your power windows not working properly or becoming stuck. Check the wiring connections, fuses, and window switches to identify the problem. The power window motor might need to be replaced if these components are in good operating order.
- wiring issues Numerous electrical issues in your car might be brought on by faulty wiring. Check the connectors and wiring harnesses for evidence of damage, such as frayed or loose connections. If any wiring problems are discovered, fix or replace the faulty wiring to guarantee proper electrical operation.
- ineffective central locking A broken actuator, faulty wiring, or a problem with the control module could be to blame if your central locking system is unable to lock or unlock the doors. Examine the fuse connected to the central locking system to start troubleshooting. To identify the root of the problem, additional research may be needed if the fuse is intact.
- light fading or flickering Numerous things, such as a weak battery, a broken alternator, unsecured wire connections, or malfunctioning light bulbs, might result in dim or flickering lights. Start by examining the battery voltage and the output of the alternator. To fix the dull or flickering lights if these parts are working properly, check the wiring connections and replace any defective bulbs.

Steps to Diagnose and Repair Car Electrical Issues

Follow these methods to accurately diagnose and fix automotive electrical problems:

Examination of battery voltage and problem-solving Start by using a multimeter to check the battery voltage. Replace or recharge the battery if necessary if the voltage is low. Additionally, look for corrosion or loose connections on the battery terminals and connectors that could prevent normal electrical flow.

Performance assessment of the alternator Using a multimeter, determine the alternator's output voltage. Make that the output is within the acceptable range. To stop battery drain and electrical issues, the alternator may need to be replaced if it is not producing enough power.

Inspection and maintenance of starter motors Make sure the starter motor connections are clean and secure by looking at them. Examine the starter motor for any symptoms of deterioration or wear. To ensure good engine starting, the starter motor may need to be replaced if it is malfunctioning.

Inspection and replacement of spark plugs Check the spark plugs for wear indicators like carbon buildup or corroded electrodes. To maintain optimum engine efficiency, replace any damaged spark plugs in accordance with the manufacturer's instructions.

replacement and testing of the ignition switch Turn the key to the ignition switch and watch what happens. To ensure effective starting, a certified automotive technician may need to replace the switch if it is non-responsive or shows signs of failure.

examination and repair of wiring Look for any indications of damage or loose connections by thoroughly inspecting the wire harnesses and connectors. To verify that the vehicle's electrical system is operating properly, fix or replace any damaged wiring.

Following component-specific troubleshooting procedures, individual electrical components, including power windows or central locking systems, are repaired. This could entail evaluating wire connections, testing switches, checking fuses, and, if necessary, replacing broken parts.

Preventive Maintenance Tips

Take into account the following preventative maintenance advice to reduce the likelihood of automotive electrical issues:

1. Battery terminals should be regularly inspected and cleaned to avoid corrosion and guarantee a reliable connection.
2. Drive the car frequently to keep the battery charged, especially on short excursions where the battery might not fully recharge.
3. A multimeter should be used to frequently check the battery's voltage and replace it if necessary.
4. According to the manufacturer's instructions, check spark plugs for wear and damage and replace them if necessary.
5. Keep the connections at the alternator and starter motor clean and tight.
6. Examine and fix any broken connectors or wiring harnesses on a regular basis.
7. In case a fuse is faulty, check it and replace it.
8. Follow the suggested maintenance schedule for your car, which should include routine electrical system repair.

When to Seek Professional Help

While some auto electrical problems can be resolved with do-it-yourself diagnostics and fixes, other circumstances could call for the skills of a qualified automotive mechanic. In the following circumstances, think about contacting a professional:

- when you lack the skills, equipment, or expertise required to identify and fix electrical issues.
- if the electrical problem requires sophisticated diagnostics or is complex.
- when repair and troubleshooting efforts fail to solve the issue.
- Consult reputable servicing facilities if the car is still covered by the warranty.

Keep in mind that only trained professionals are equipped with the knowledge and tools necessary to correctly identify and fix complex electrical system issues in vehicles.

For a car to remain in good working order, it is crucial to comprehend the various parts of the electrical system, be aware of frequent electrical problems' symptoms, and use efficient troubleshooting strategies. By using the procedures described in this blog post, you may identify and fix automotive electrical issues, resulting in a comfortable ride and a dependable electrical system. The lifetime and ideal performance of your vehicle's electrical system will be enhanced by routine preventative maintenance and obtaining professional assistance when necessary.

Chapter 5:

Cooling System

The radiator and the thermostat assembly make up the two components of the engine cooling system. In the top part of the engine, there is a thermostat that resembles a valve. When temperatures rise over a specific level, the thermostat opens to let coolant flow. Below this temperature, it closes to prevent coolant flow back into the radiator when the engine temperature falls below that level. It's common to refer to the thermostat as a "cooling fan." A faulty thermostat might result in significant coolant loss from water pouring out of the engine.

The radiator and any other components used to move heat away from the engine make up the cooling system in addition to the thermostat. A common cause of cooling-system failure is mechanical damage, overheating, or poor maintenance. Because it enables correct temperature regulation for typical vehicle operation, the cooling system plays a crucial role in vehicle operation.

Along with overheating, the cooling system may develop mineral buildup that hinders heat transfer. Numerous engine issues are caused by insufficient cooling.

Radiator

The radiator's primary job is to cool the engine by dissipating heat from the hot coolant inside the engine and releasing it into the cooler outside air. A forced-air cooled radiator is standard in most cars. The engine is the primary heat source in a car's cooling system. By exchanging it with the air around, this heat can be controlled on a budget. In order to exchange coolant's heat with the heat of the surrounding air, the cooling system uses the radiator, a heat exchanger made up of tubes through which coolant travels. In a normal radiator, coolant enters from the bottom and rises through a network of tubes that form the radiator's outer shell. The "coolant pipe"—the fluid that emerges from the radiator—flows via the thermostat-controlled tube between the thermostat housing and the radiator to enter the engine. Water pumps, or fans, are the aggregate name for the tubes in the engine block that provide this flow's pathways.

A lack of hot coolant may prevent appropriate cooling if a cooling system malfunctions, such as a broken thermostat, blocked air filter box, or a bypass hose. The engine may overheat in these circumstances, leading to failure or internal component damage. Overheating is a state that should never be allowed to occur.

The radiator is an important part of the cooling system because it moves heat from the engine to the coolant and then removes that heat from the car through the outside air to allow it to cool. Without a radiator, an engine could lose a lot of cooling fluid, which could result in major harm or even a breakdown of the vehicle.

As coolant circulates through an engine cooling system, water and air are exchanged.

More water than air is present in the engine when it is cold. "Hydrostatic pressure" refers to the combination of water and air. By flowing over the hot portions of the engine and radiator, the coolant dissipates heat and prevents overheating as a result of being forced out of its passageways by the pressure. Your radiator will be filled with coolant on a hot day after you have just shifted into drive. The pressure of hot gases can force coolant out of leaks in the cooling system when the engine warms up because it contains more air than water. Your radiator won't be fully charged as a result on a hot day.

A larger coolant to air ratio is present when the engine is cold. The cold air's pressure pushes it up against hot surfaces, causing heat loss. In order to produce cooling, the higher pressure of hot gases in a cold engine forces them into cooler spaces, such the radiator.

Look underneath the car and listen for leaks to find cooling system leaks quickly. You can also use a hose to apply a continuous spray of water to suspected hoses and connections. Although effective, these techniques could cost you some coolant. A pressure gauge test of your cooling system's pressure is an additional method. Finding out what kind of cooling system your car has will help you achieve this. Every car ought to have a sticker in the engine compartment that identifies the type of cooling system it has.

Ask your mechanic if you are uncertain. You may get a specialist radiator pressure tester from any auto parts store after you are aware of the type of cooling system your vehicle has. Depending on your car, the gauge is placed within the radiator cap on top or the side, and it displays pressure measurements in either pounds per square inch (psi) or bar measurement units. Verify that the gauge is never submerged in water. A leak may be present if the gauge reads close to zero rather than at zero, which indicates that the system is operating at normal pressure. If the pressure in your radiator cap is higher than 30 psi under typical circumstances, your cooling system most likely has a minor leak.

Using an electronic pressure testing kit, system pressure can also be checked. Any gadget for the vehicle's electronic tuning or electrical system diagnostics can be used for this. The pressure reading is the end consequence of locating cooling system leaks.

Because it has no or little protection from overheating, a leaky radiator cap may indicate a problem with the cooling system. However, a leak is not usually detected by pressure measurement. A leak in one area of the system could result in pressure that is normal for that area of the system but still insufficient to damage another area when it fails later.

If the pressure is low and not zero, there is a leak in the system, which is something that automobiles do not enjoy. There is a good chance that a leak will start if the pressure falls below normal levels, further harming the system's other components. Therefore, replacing or repairing a radiator cap or any other component of your cooling system is essential for an efficient cooling system because doing so fixes all leaks simultaneously.

In order to ensure optimal operation, cooling systems need to be frequently maintained and examined. By doing this, the system is protected from harm and any necessary leak repairs are made. An engine might overheat and break down if a cooling system isn't kept up with.

Every two years or 5000 miles, coolant should be replaced. Only particular temperatures are designed to be safe for the fluid used in cooling systems. The coolant is pumped into the engine at a high heat because water is good up to 212°F and above. It naturally warms up as the engine starts up and cools down as it runs. Coolant leaks are prevented by the kill switch in the radiator, which prevents water from escaping.

Bleeding the cooling system's air should be done to remove air from it. This is carried out to ensure that any air bubbles in the radiator are expelled from the system and that any harm brought on by air that is trapped in a radiator or hoses is prevented. You can use a radiator bleeding kit or a pressure bleeder, which is less expensive but takes more time and requires a steady hand, to get rid of air bubbles. Consult your vehicle's owner's manual for instructions if you are unsure of how to bleed your car.

How to check the cooling system pressure to maintain proper operation and prevent further significant damage.

The radiator pressure tester's dropper end should be inserted into the radiator cap located above your engine. Never submerge the gauge when testing since it could shatter. In pounds per square inch (PSI) or bars, the gauge will show the reading. If the gauge reads more over 30 psi, there is a leak and you should take your vehicle to your mechanic so they can examine the system.

Utilizing an electronic pressure tester is a more accurate approach to check the system pressure in your car. Any gadget for your vehicle's electrical system diagnostics or electronic tuning can be used for this. The pressure tester will display you an overall reading and a visual representation of how much air was found in the cooling system, letting you know the state of your cooling system.

The gauge readings may indicate coolant system leaks if they are low, but this method is not particularly dependable. It is advised to use a radiator pressure tester as a substitute due to this ambiguity.

It's crucial to frequently check your antifreeze levels and maintain them full because it stops corrosion. Parts of cooling systems might develop cracks due to corrosion, which can weaken metal. By thoroughly checking the coolant level in your car and topping it out as necessary, you can prevent this.

It's critical to prevent rust on your engine at all times, but this is especially true when it's operating at full capacity. The metal components of cars and other vehicles are protected by corrosion inhibitors, which are present in many coolants. These corrosion inhibitors stop corrosion and shield the metal from the destructive heat produced by an engine by adhering to the metal's surface.

Steps for Repairing an Engine Coolant Level

- ❖ Be prepared with a heavy-duty jack and jack stand.
- ❖ Drain the transmission oil by removing the plug. To prevent dirt buildup, add a small amount of oil to the engine.
- ❖ To avoid an electrical short, cut the battery cable. If your coolant solution contains corrosion inhibitors that could react with an electrical source and start a fire, this may also be necessary.
- ❖ Verify that the radiator's level is full by removing the level gauge. A measuring cup can be used for this.
- ❖ To remove the dipstick from the engine, raise the hook on the dipstick. Before reintroducing it into the engine, be certain that a new level is in place.
- ❖ A little bit more than halfway between the level and the top of the reservoir, pour coolant into the overflow area. Coolant overflow leaks will result from pouring coolant above this mark.
- ❖ Reattach the negative battery cable and the radiator cap.
- ❖ As directed in your owner's handbook, fill the engine with water and coolant. For further information regarding the amount of coolant required for your particular vehicle, consult your owner's handbook.
- ❖ Launch the car, let it idle for a while, and then shut off the engine. Verify that there are no leaks at this moment.

❖ As directed in your owner's manual, replenish the engine with water and coolant as necessary.

It's time to inspect and fix your cooling system if you see any droplets or spills of radiator fluid. Contact your mechanic as soon as a leak is discovered so that it may be fixed and the system can be shielded from harm. Please contact us for a consultation if you'd want further details on correcting an engine coolant level.

An automobile's cooling system uses coolant to keep the engine cool. Together, the radiator and fan aid in the coolant's circulation throughout your engine. The combustion process produces heat, which the coolant aids in dissipating. To ensure that your cooling system is operating properly, coolant should be added on a regular basis. An automobile's cooling system uses coolant to keep the engine cool. Together, the radiator and fan aid in the coolant's circulation throughout your engine. The combustion process produces heat, which the coolant aids in dissipating. To ensure that your cooling system is operating properly, coolant should be added on a regular basis.

Replacing The Coolant

This is a crucial step in keeping your car in good condition and can prevent costly issues. The coolant in your engine can eventually leak out of the system if you don't keep it maintained, which will harm your car.

Once every two to three years, coolant needs to be added to your cooling system. It can cost thousands of dollars to fix a coolant leak after it occurs and to fix any problems that resulted from the leak in the first place. In order to prevent harm to your car from a leak, the coolant that is added to the cooling system should be done by a professional.

All vehicles follow the same process for adding coolant and combining it with the already-installed coolant. Along with a fresh batch of coolant, the components for mixing coolant are frequently provided. It is crucial to be aware of the numerous types of mixers that some vehicles may have in order to avoid using the incorrect part and inadvertently damaging your vehicle. The owner's manual should be consulted for information on how to check the coolant level and where to add it.

Checking your car's coolant promptly can enable you to get it fixed right away if you are experiencing engine overheating issues. If a leak is discovered in your cooling system, you might want to contact your insurance provider to see if they will pay for any necessary repairs. An antifreeze leak is present if you spot any orange or green leaks. Your engine will corrode as a result, and it will cost roughly $4,000 to fix.

Tips for Adding Coolant

To prevent reactions that could harm your car, always go by the guidelines that are included with your coolant.

- ❖ Place cold coolant in at all times. This will lessen the likelihood of harming an engine component.
- ❖ Never mix hot coolant with current coolant since the mixture may foam or bubble, which could damage components or result in other issues.
- ❖ Avoid using too much coolant. This can harm your engine and end up costing more in the long term to fix.
- ❖ Mixing various coolant kinds can seriously harm your car, so never do it.

To make sure your engine cooling system is in good working order, coolant should be changed every three years or 60,000 miles. You can notice a leak in your automobile as a result of a coolant leak if you don't change your coolant frequently enough.

Chapter 6:

Air Conditioning System

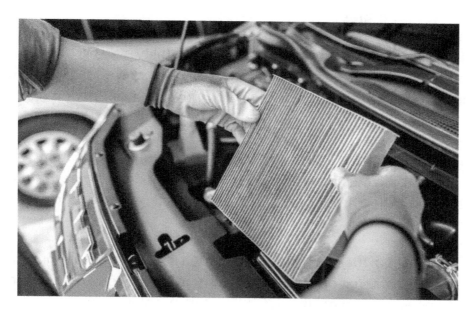

system is essential, especially when the temperatures rise in the summer. Uncomfortable conditions, potential health risks, and expensive repairs might result from neglecting the A/C system. This article will examine the significance of maintaining your air conditioning system and offer helpful information on typical A/C repair issues.

Understanding the Car's A/C System

Air cooling system components The compressor, condenser, evaporator, expansion valve, and refrigerant are some of the essential parts of the air conditioning system. Each part is essential to the vehicle's cooling and air circulation.

Workings of the A/C system Heat transmission is the basis for how the A/C system operates. A specialized fluid called refrigerant cools down the cabin air by absorbing heat from it. The car is then re-circulated with the cooled air to make driving more comfortable.

importance of the A/C system operating properly By keeping the right temperature inside the car, a well working A/C system guarantees a comfortable trip. Additionally, by controlling the interior temperature, a well-maintained A/C system helps avoid health problems like heat exhaustion.

Signs of A/C System Issues

No air coming out of the vents or hot air The inability to chill the air or a lack of airflow from the vents are two of the most typical indications of an A/C system problem. This can be the result of a broken compressor, a refrigerant leak, or a system clog.

A/C system noises that are unusual Strange sounds emanating from the air conditioning system, such as screeching, rattling, or grinding, point to potential issues. These noises could be the result of a broken fan belt, a malfunctioning compressor, or loose parts.

Odd smells when using the air conditioner When the A/C is running, musty or foul smells may indicate bacterial or mold growth within the system. By utilizing the proper cleaning solutions and cleaning the A/C filter, this problem can be solved.

weakened cooling or reduced airflow It may be an indication of problems like clogged filters, a broken fan, or low refrigerant levels if the airflow from the vents is insufficient or the cooling is less efficient than before.

Troubleshooting and Diagnosing A/C System Problems

examining the airflow and fans It's essential to check the fans and airflow for any obstructions or technical problems that can have an impact on how well the A/C system works. This entails inspecting the fan motor, fan blades, and related wiring.

checking the components of the A/C compressor The refrigerant is pressurized and circulated by the air conditioner compressor. The appropriate operation of the compressor, clutch, and drive belt is ensured by a careful examination, which also reveals any indications of damage or wear.

testing the electric clutch and wiring The A/C system may malfunction due to faulty wiring or a broken electric clutch. By testing the electrical parts, you can make sure they're working properly and find any problems with the wiring or clutch.

finding air conditioning system leaks The performance of the A/C system might be considerably impacted by refrigerant leakage. Professionals can find leaks and fix them to restore the system's effectiveness using specialized equipment and methods.

recognizing low coolant levels as a frequent problem Leaks or poor maintenance can cause low coolant levels. To keep the A/C system performing at its best, this problem must be identified and fixed.

Safety Precautions for Car A/C Repair

importance of safety glasses and gloves Prioritizing safety is vital when working on the A/C system. Gloves and safety glasses offer protection from possible damage and exposure to dangerous chemicals.

proper chemical handling, storage, and disposal Careful adherence to storage and disposal instructions is required when handling chemicals, including refrigerants. To protect the environment and public health, these compounds should be kept in a secure place and disposed of correctly.

DIY A/C System Repairs

refrigerant recharging the air conditioning system The cooling capacity of the A/C system can be recovered by adding fresh refrigerant. However, it's crucial to use the proper refrigerant kind and quantity and to adhere to the manufacturer's instructions.

replacing hoses for the air conditioner that have been harmed A/C hoses may deteriorate or start to leak over time. Replacing these hoses guarantees correct refrigerant flow and averts further AC system problems.

Changing or cleaning the air conditioning filter Maintaining optimal air quality inside the car requires regularly cleaning or replacing the A/C filter. Airflow might be hampered and disagreeable scents can be exacerbated by a filthy or clogged filter.

resolving typical electrical problems Electrical problems may be the cause of some A/C system troubles. Common electrical issues like defective wiring or a broken electric clutch can be fixed in order to fix the A/C system.

When to Seek Professional Help

specialist knowledge and equipment are needed for complex repairs. A/C system repairs that involve complex electrical issues or the replacement of significant components, for example, need for the skills of experts with specialized training and tools.

Repairing leaks in the system and recharging Recharging the A/C system and finding and fixing refrigerant leaks are tasks that should only be performed by qualified experts. They are equipped and trained to handle refrigerants safely.

AC compressor replacement It need technical know-how to replace the A/C compressor because it is a complicated process. Professional installation and successful operation of the new compressor can be guaranteed.

Preventive Maintenance Tips

A/C system checks and upkeep on a regular basis Regular A/C system maintenance and inspections help to spot any problems before they become more serious. This include inspecting for leaks, cleaning the parts, and checking the levels of the refrigerant.

The necessity of cleaning the evaporator and condenser coils Over time, dirt and debris can build up on the condenser and evaporator coils, reducing the efficiency of the A/C system. Cleaning these coils on a regular basis guarantees ideal heat transfer and ventilation.

replacement and inspection of the cabin air filter To keep the air inside the car clean, the cabin air filter is essential. Pollutants like pollen and dust are kept out of the cabin by routinely inspecting and replacing the filter.

Keeping obstacles and trash out of the A/C system The appropriate airflow and prevention of potential damage are promoted by routinely checking the area around the A/C system and removing any debris or obstacles, such as leaves or debris in the condenser unit.

Common Myths and Misconceptions About AC Systems

Only refrigerant levels affect cooling effectiveness. While refrigerant levels are crucial, the total cooling effectiveness of the A/C system also depends on other elements including correct airflow, working parts, and sufficient insulation.

It is dangerous to use the A/C system in the winter. By keeping seals and components from drying out throughout the winter, running the A/C system helps maintain its functionality. Additionally, it helps keep the cabin at a reasonable temperature and defogs the windows.

Increasing the refrigerant will resolve all AC problems. Without addressing the underlying problem, adding refrigerant can provide momentary respite but does not eliminate the problem. To ensure that the A/C system will perform properly over the long term, the specific issue must be identified and fixed.

Benefits of Maintaining a Healthy A/C System

increased comfort in hotter climates Driving is more comfortable and enjoyable when the A/C system is working properly, especially in hot weather. It contributes to temperature control, preventing discomfort and weariness.

improved air quality within the car Cleaner air inside the car is guaranteed by routine A/C system maintenance, including filter cleaning or replacement. As a result, contaminants and allergens are less prevalent and the air quality is improved.

keeping expensive repairs and component deterioration at bay Prioritizing A/C system maintenance allows drivers to spot potential problems early and take action, avoiding more involved and expensive repairs in the future. Regular maintenance helps A/C system components last longer and prevents further harm.

Maintenance is crucial to ensuring the longevity and effectiveness of the air conditioning system. For the A/C system to last as long as possible and operate at its best, regular maintenance is crucial. A well-functioning A/C system is a result of routine inspections, prompt repairs, and preventative actions.

urging drivers to prioritize A/C system maintenance for an enjoyable and safe summer driving experience Prioritizing A/C system maintenance is essential, especially in the summer, to provide a safe and comfortable driving experience. Drivers can take advantage of a well-running A/C system that delivers cool air circulation and maximum comfort during their journeys by adhering to the suggested preventive measures and obtaining professional assistance when necessary.

Chapter 7:

Braking System

When it comes to vehicle safety, a properly working braking system is crucial. The braking system makes sure you can stop your car quickly and safely, avoiding collisions and retaining control on the road. We'll go into the nuances of the braking system in this blog post, including its parts, common problems, maintenance advice, and even the prospect of changing your braking system. Understanding how the braking system functions will help you take better care of your automobile and make decisions about brake upgrades and repairs.

How the Braking System Works

The braking system is a sophisticated set of parts that work together to transform your car's kinetic energy into heat, which either slows it down or brings it to a complete stop. Let's investigate the fundamental parts of a standard braking system:

1. **Brake pedal:** The driver utilizes the brake pedal as an input device to engage the braking system.

2. **Master cylinder:** In order to transmit hydraulic pressure to the braking system, the master cylinder converts the force supplied to the brake pedal into hydraulic pressure.
3. **Brake fluid:** Within the braking system, hydraulic pressure is delivered through the medium of brake fluid. It is essential for effective brake operation.
4. **Brake lines and hoses:** Brake hoses and lines transfer brake fluid from the master cylinder to the various parts of the braking system, including the calipers and wheel cylinders.
5. **Calipers and wheel cylinders:** The appropriate pressure is applied to the brake shoes or pads by calipers and wheel cylinders, creating the friction required to slow down or stop the vehicle.
6. **Brake pads and shoes:** The parts that come into direct contact with the rotors and drums to produce friction and slow the vehicle down are brake shoes for drum brakes and brake pads for disc brakes.
7. **Rotors and drums:** The revolving parts that the brake shoes or pads press up against to generate friction are called rotors (for disc brakes) and drums (for drum brakes).
8. **Brake sensors and ABS system:** For optimum performance, brake sensors keep an eye on the braking system's many components, including wheel speed. The Anti-lock Braking System (ABS) is a safety feature that improves control and stability by preventing wheel lock-up during emergency braking.

A dual-circuit braking system is another option for the braking system. This technology divides the braking system into two independent hydraulic circuits to offer redundancy and improve safety. Here are the main characteristics of a dual-circuit braking system:

1. A dual-circuit braking system's description and function: Two distinct hydraulic circuits, each in charge of stopping two wheels, make up the dual-circuit braking system. Because of this layout, even if one circuit fails, the other will continue to function partially as a brake.
2. Master and slave cylinder operation: The master cylinder is split into two parts, each of which is connected to a separate hydraulic circuit. When the brake pedal is depressed, the master cylinder's two portions are activated, supplying hydraulic pressure to the corresponding circuits.
3. The slave cylinders in the calipers or wheel cylinders receive the hydraulic pressure generated by the master cylinder and exert force as a result. By

applying force to the rotors or drums in response to this pressure, the brake shoes or pads help the vehicle stop.

4. The braking system can continue to function even if one of the two hydraulic circuits fails because to the dual-circuit design's redundancy. In the event of a component failure, this redundancy increases safety and offers a backup.

5. Dual-circuit braking systems frequently include mechanisms to change the rear brake power distribution to maximize braking effectiveness. These include a load-sensitive pressure-limiting valve and a rear brake power adjustment. Additionally, load-sensitive pressure-limiting valves are used to control brake pressure based on the weight of the vehicle, ensuring constant braking performance under a variety of circumstances.

6. How anti-lock braking systems (ABS) work: Modern safety elements called Anti-lock Braking Systems (ABS) guard against wheel lock-up in emergency braking scenarios. The ABS technology greatly improves the stability and safety of the vehicle by modulating the brake pressure to each wheel independently, allowing the driver to maintain steering control even when applying heavy braking.

Common Brake System Issues

Over time, brake systems might experience problems even with routine maintenance. It's crucial to be aware of the typical symptoms and warning signals that point to probable braking system issues. Here are some typical problems with brake systems to look out for:

Brake system warning signs and symptoms:

1. Squeaking or grinding noises: When applying the brakes, strange noises like squeaking or grinding may be a sign of worn brake shoes or pads. It's essential to take care of this problem right away to stop future damage and guarantee optimum braking performance.

2. Vibration or pulsation in the brake pedal: When braking, pulsations or vibrations in the brake pedal may indicate warped brake rotors. To maintain efficient and smooth braking, warped rotors should be repaired as they might compromise braking efficiency.

3. Soft or spongy brake pedal: When the brake pedal is squeezed, if it feels spongy or mushy, there may be air in the brake lines or a possible brake fluid leak. To

maintain appropriate brake operation, a soft brake pedal needs to be addressed immediately.

4. Brake fluid leaks: Deteriorated brake lines or bad seals can cause brake fluid leakage. To avoid brake failure, any indications of brake fluid leaks, such as damp spots close to the wheels or under the car, should be taken care of right away.

5. Warning lights on the dashboard: Modern cars include dashboard warning lights that come on when the brake system notices something out of the ordinary. To find and fix the root of the problem, it's essential to pay attention to these warning lights and have the system checked by a specialist.

Common causes of brake system problems:

1. Worn brake pads or shoes: Brake shoes or pads must be replaced as they become worn out over time from friction. Failure to replace worn brake shoes or pads can result in reduced stopping power and possibly even damage to other braking system parts.

2. Brake fluid contamination or depletion: Brake fluid that is contaminated or depleted can cause lower stopping power and possibly harm hydraulic parts. As advised by the manufacturer, brake fluid should be routinely checked and changed.

3. Malfunctioning brake calipers or wheel cylinders: The ability of brake calipers and wheel cylinders to apply consistent pressure to the brake pads or shoes might suffer from problems like sticking or leaking. To maintain proper brake operation, damaged calipers or cylinders should be fixed or replaced.

4. Rotor or drum damage: Brake rotors or drums that are warped or broken might create pulsations, vibrations, or uneven braking. To regain optimal braking performance, damaged rotors or drums may need to be resurfaced or replaced.

5. Faulty ABS sensors or control module: ABS warning lights and potential problems with the ABS system's functionality can result from ABS sensors failing or the control module malfunctioning. To guarantee that this safety system operates as intended, proper ABS component diagnosis and maintenance are crucial.

Brake System Maintenance

For maximum performance and safety, braking system maintenance must be performed regularly. By performing routine maintenance, you may increase the lifespan of your braking system and identify any problems early. The following are some essential components of brake system upkeep:

➢ Importance of regular brake system maintenance: Regular brake system maintenance ensures dependable braking performance and reduces the need for expensive repairs by allowing possible problems to be identified and addressed early on. Additionally, it enhances overall car safety.
➢ Brake inspection and servicing intervals: Regular brake inspections ought to be carried out at the intervals advised by the manufacturer. This normally entails examining the state of brake parts, measuring the thickness of brake shoes and pads, testing the quantity and quality of brake fluid, and evaluating overall braking effectiveness.

DIY brake maintenance tips:

1. Checking brake fluid level and condition: Check the brake fluid level and condition on a regular basis. Cleanliness, contamination-free conditions, and the recommended level of brake fluid are required. If required, top off the brake fluid or have a professional replenish it.
2. Inspecting brake pads and shoes: To make sure they are within the advised ranges, measure the thickness of the brake shoes and pads. To preserve optimal braking performance and prevent damage to other components, replace worn brake shoes or pads as away.
3. Cleaning and lubricating brake components: To get rid of dirt and debris, clean the slides, pins, and calipers on the brakes. To ensure smooth operation and avoid sticking, lubricate the necessary components with brake-specific lubricants.
4. Flushing and bleeding the brake system: According to the manufacturer's guidelines, brake fluid should be frequently cleansed and changed. By flushing the brake system, old fluid and pollutants are removed, preserving optimal hydraulic operation.

Professional brake system servicing:

1. Brake system inspection by a certified technician: Professional brake system checks performed by licensed experts offer a comprehensive evaluation of brake system parts, ensuring possible problems are found and fixed. This includes determining brake pad wear, evaluating the state of the rotor or drum, inspecting the hydraulic parts, and determining how the ABS system is functioning.
2. Brake pad/shoe replacement: Brake shoes or pads that have worn past the advised limits should be replaced by a qualified technician. For the best braking performance, quality parts and proper installation are essential.
3. Rotor or drum resurfacing or replacement: Resurfacing or replacement may be required if brake rotors or drums are broken or worn beyond the permissible levels. This guarantees a smooth braking surface and appropriate engagement of the brake shoes or pads.
4. Brake fluid flush and replacement: Professional brake fluid flushes involve draining out the old fluid, flushing in new fluid, and making sure the system is properly bled to get rid of any air pockets. The best brake system performance is maintained thanks to this procedure.
5. ABS system diagnosis and repair: Any problems with the ABS system, such as defective sensors, control module problems, or ABS warning lights, can be identified and fixed by certified personnel. Correct repair and accurate diagnosis guarantee that the ABS system works efficiently to increase vehicle safety.

Upgrading Your Braking System

You could think about updating your braking system if you need increased stopping power or have particular requirements. You have a variety of alternatives to improve your car's braking power:

Performance brake pads and rotors:

1. Benefits and considerations: Performance brake rotors and pads provide greater durability, less brake fade, and improved stopping power. They are made to withstand higher temperatures and offer more reliable performance in difficult driving situations. They could be noisier and could emit more dust than regular brake parts, though.
2. Types of performance brake pads and rotors: Performance brake pads and rotors come in a variety of materials, including as ceramic, semi-metallic, and

drilled or slotted rotors. It's important to select the best option based on your driving tastes and the needs of the vehicle because each type has different benefits and factors to take into account.

Stainless steel brake lines:

1. Advantages of stainless steel brake lines: Compared to traditional rubber brake lines, stainless steel brake lines are more durable, resist corrosion, and expand less. They give the brake pedal a harder feel and support steady brake pressure, particularly during harsh braking.
2. Installation process and considerations: Replace the current rubber brake lines with stainless steel ones when upgrading to stainless steel brake lines. It's essential to make sure the installation is done correctly, and the upgrade should be done by a qualified expert.

Performance brake fluid:

1. Benefits of performance brake fluid: As a result of their higher boiling points than regular brake fluids, performance brake fluids lessen the possibility of brake fade under difficult driving situations. They offer improved thermal stability and support consistent braking operation.
2. Considerations and compatibility: It's crucial to select a performance brake fluid that is compatible with the requirements of your car's braking system. When in doubt, heed the manufacturer's advice and seek advice from a specialist.

Understanding how the brake system works, how to maintain it, and what enhancements could be possible is crucial for responsible vehicle ownership. The best braking performance may be ensured and expensive repairs can be avoided with the help of routine brake system checks, rapid attention to warning indicators, and adherence to maintenance intervals. It's critical to select brake system upgrades that are compatible with your driving preferences, the needs of your vehicle, and safety considerations. Examples of such upgrades include performance brake pads, rotors, stainless steel brake lines, and performance brake fluid. You can help make driving safer and more pleasurable by taking good care of your car's braking system.

Chapter 8:

Exhaust System

A vehicle's exhaust system is essential for both performance and emission control. It is in charge of safely venting the reaction exhaust gases into the environment and directing them away from the engine. An overview of the exhaust system and why it matters is given below:

1. Components: The exhaust system is made up of a number of parts, including:
    - Exhaust manifold: Gathers engine cylinder exhaust gases.
    - If present, a turbocharger boosts engine power by compressing incoming air.
    - Using a catalytic converter, toxic gases are changed into less dangerous chemicals, hence reducing air pollution.
    - Silencer/Muffler: Lessens noise caused by exhaust gases.
    - Releases exhaust gases outside the car through the tailpipe.
2. Functionality: The exhaust system serves a number of purposes, including:
    - Exhaust gas direction: It prevents hot exhaust gases from entering the passenger area by directing them away from the engine.

- Noise reduction: The engine's combustion process generates noise, which is reduced by the muffler or silencer.
- Catalytic converters are used in engines to limit emissions of dangerous pollutants such carbon monoxide, nitrogen oxides, and hydrocarbons (CO).

3. Importance in performance: By increasing exhaust gas flow, an improved exhaust system can improve a vehicle's performance. It makes it possible for the engine to remove combustion byproducts more effectively, which may result in greater power being produced.

4. Importance in emission control: The catalytic converter in particular, found in the exhaust system, is crucial in lowering air pollution. Before toxic gases are released into the atmosphere, they can be changed chemically in the catalytic converter into less damaging chemicals.

5. Regulations: Various agencies have established standards governing vehicle exhaust emissions. These rules, such as EURO 5 in Europe or BS-4 in India, specify the maximum quantities of pollutants that are allowed to be emitted by cars. To guarantee that environmental criteria are met, the exhaust system must abide by these rules.

The information presented above is only a comprehensive review of the exhaust system and its significance, thus it is significant to keep in mind. Depending on the vehicle's make, model, and the regional regulatory regulations in effect, specifics may change.

Common Causes of Exhaust System Problems

1. Loose Gas Cap: Fuel vapors can escape from the tank due to a loose gas cap, resulting in emissions problems and perhaps turning on the Check Engine light. Additionally, it may result in pollutants and dirt getting into the engine's fuel, decreasing performance.

2. Dirty Air Filter: Before it reaches the engine, dirt and debris are captured by the air filter of a car. The engine may sputter or misfire when the air filter is dirty because it may function less effectively and let debris in.

3. Faulty Catalytic Converter: The catalytic converter is essential for eliminating dangerous exhaust gases. Inaccurate emissions measurements and poor vehicle performance might result from the catalytic converter being clogged or not

working properly. The engine may misfire or have performance troubles, and the Check Engine light may come on.

4. Bad Oxygen Sensors: To ensure the correct air-fuel ratio, oxygen sensors analyze the oxygen levels in the exhaust. Oxygen sensors may not effectively gauge the exhaust emission levels if one or more of them malfunction or stop working, which can cause performance problems including engine misfires or higher fuel usage.

5. Exhaust Leaks: Strong points in the exhaust system, such as joints, might crack due to rough road conditions and other circumstances, allowing deadly gases to escape into the passenger cabin. Risks to one's health and safety can result from this. It's crucial to seek the help of a qualified mechanic if the exhaust system shows signs of a leak or break.

These are a few of the typical reasons why exhaust systems malfunction. To preserve the exhaust system's proper operation and to guarantee vehicle performance and safety, it's critical to fix these problems right away.

Diagnosing and Fixing Exhaust System Problems

There are various typical difficulties that may surface during the diagnosis and repair of exhaust system issues. For each of the following issues, I will offer recommendations and step-by-step instructions:

Checking for Loose Gas Cap:

- Knowing the dangers of a malfunctioning muffler is the first step in inspecting the gas cap. A damaged muffler can allow harmful gases like carbon monoxide to seep into the car's interior, causing health risks and even resulting in fines or service denial.
- Pay attention to your car's sound because a damaged muffler could make it sound louder than usual. Noises like thumps or clunking could be the result of a damaged exhaust system part.
- Lift the automobile using a car jack, then check the muffler for rust and holes. Visible rust on the outside could be a sign of a more serious issue inside. A sign that rust-caused holes have formed in the muffler is water dripping from it.

- It is advised that you send your automobile to a professional for a more thorough examination and any required repairs if you suspect a faulty exhaust system.

Cleaning or Replacing Air Filter

- The air filter is essential for preserving the best engine performance. Regular replacement or cleaning is crucial.
- Open the air filter housing and take the filter out to clean it. Use compressed air to blow the dust out after gently tapping the filter to clear any loose material. Avoid using liquid or water-based cleansers. Reinstall the filter after cleaning.
- It is advised to replace the air filter if it is damaged or overly unclean. For information on how to replace an air filter specifically, consult your car's owner's manual. In addition to ensuring optimal engine performance, routine air filter cleaning helps keep junk out of the fuel and exhaust systems.

Testing and Repairing the Catalytic Converter

- The catalytic converter is in charge of cutting back on dangerous pollutants. If it is broken, there are ways to identify the problem.
- The presence of the Check Engine light may signal a catalytic converter issue. A mechanic can use diagnostic tools to search for error codes and do additional tests to verify the problem.
- A catalytic converter is frequently beyond economical repair and must be replaced. It is advised to take your car to a mechanic for advice if you think your catalytic converter may be malfunctioning.

Replacing Oxygen Sensors

- Oxygen sensors are used to assess emissions and guarantee optimum air/fuel ratios. Replace them if they're broken if they are.
- Track down the oxygen sensors in your car. They are normally found before and after the catalytic converter throughout the exhaust system.
- Using a suitable wrench or socket, unplug the electrical connector and remove the old sensor. Connect the electrical connector after replacing the oxygen sensor. Make sure the sensor is securely fastened, but don't tighten it too much.

- To make sure that the new oxygen sensors you choose will work with your exact make and model of car, check the handbook or a reputable parts supplier.

Identifying and Fixing Exhaust Leaks

- Although exhaust leaks might be problematic, there are ways to find and fix them.
- Check the exhaust system for any strange noises or hissing that can point to a leak. Check the area around the connectors and joints for exhaust fumes.
- Visually examine the exhaust system for soot, dark stains, or frayed connections. Check concealed spots with a flashlight as well.
- You could require supplies like exhaust sealant, exhaust tape, or replacement gaskets to address exhaust leaks. The location and severity of the leak will determine the repair strategy. It is advised to seek expert assistance if the repair is difficult or requires welding.

Always put safety first and seek the advice of a qualified mechanic when dealing with complicated exhaust system issues or if you have questions about any of the procedures involved.

Chapter 9:

The Traditional Fuel System

Maintaining your car's fuel system is essential for optimum performance and long-term financial benefits. You can make sure that your conventional fuel system operates properly and efficiently by being aware of its parts and doing routine maintenance. In this post, we'll look at the value of routine fuel system maintenance, examine the various parts of the conventional fuel system, go through the advantages of routine maintenance, and briefly consider alternate fuel sources. By the conclusion, you'll have a thorough comprehension of how to maintain the gasoline system in your car.

Understanding the Traditional Fuel System

History of traditional fuel cars

Let's take a quick look at the history of conventional fuel cars before getting into the significance of fuel system maintenance. Traditional fuel vehicles have been the main means of transportation for decades, running on either gasoline or diesel. The delivery of the required gasoline to the engine for combustion in these cars depends on a sophisticated fuel system. Understanding the history of conventional fuel vehicles helps us appreciate the need of keeping their fuel systems maintained.

Overview of petrol and diesel as traditional fuels

The two primary traditional fuels utilized in cars today are gasoline and diesel. Petrol is a flammable combination of hydrocarbons generated from crude oil, sometimes referred to as gasoline. Due to its better combustion properties and higher energy density, it is frequently utilized in cars and other small vehicles. Diesel fuel, on the other hand, is a heavier and less flammable fuel that is typically used in bigger vehicles like trucks and buses. Compression ignition, which is the basis for diesel engine operation, causes the fuel mixture to ignite without the use of a spark plug.

Benefits of Regular Fuel System Maintenance

Numerous advantages of keeping up with routine maintenance procedures for your car's fuel system include higher performance, increased fuel economy, cost savings, and longer engine life. Let's examine these advantages in more detail:

Enhanced performance through optimal fuel delivery

The effective and accurate distribution of fuel to the engine is ensured by a well-maintained fuel system. The fuel pump, injectors, and throttle body all work together to deliver the required fuel-air combination for combustion. Maintaining these components' integrity and functionality through routine maintenance techniques improves fuel delivery and overall vehicle performance.

Improved fuel efficiency and economy

Enhancing fuel economy through regular maintenance results in cost savings over time. Gasoline combustion is efficient and results in less wasted fuel when the fuel system is well-maintained and operating at its best. You can get more miles per gallon of fuel by doing routine maintenance procedures including fuel injector cleaning, throttle body cleaning, and fuel filter replacement.

Prevention of costly repairs and damages

Inadequate fuel system maintenance might result in serious issues and expensive future repairs. Fuel spray patterns can be affected and engine efficiency might be decreased if fuel injectors get blocked with deposits over time. An obstructed fuel flow can put stress on the fuel pump and perhaps harm the injectors. This is caused by a filthy fuel filter. Regular maintenance procedures, such as fuel system inspections and fuel tank cleaning, allow you to see possible problems early and take action to mitigate further damage and high repair costs.

Extension of engine life

The longevity of the engine in your car is considerably increased by a properly maintained fuel system. The engine receives the optimum amount of fuel and runs smoothly thanks to clean fuel injectors and a working fuel pump. You can lengthen the life of your engine and benefit from a more dependable and long-lasting car by avoiding fuel-related problems and making sure that fuel is delivered optimally.

Maintenance of warranty coverage

Maintaining the manufacturer's warranty protection requires routine fuel system repair. Failure to follow the maintenance guidelines specified in your car's owner's manual may void your warranty. You can increase your peace of mind by following the advised maintenance procedures, such as fuel quality checks and fuel system inspections, to make sure your guarantee is still in effect.

Components of the Traditional Fuel System

Learn about the numerous parts that make up the conventional fuel system in order to comprehend the nuances of fuel system maintenance. Together, these parts transport fuel from the tank to the engine for combustion. Let's quickly examine each element:

Fuel tank

In the car, the fuel is kept in the fuel tank. It is meant to withstand the corrosive properties of fuel and is often made of steel or high-density polyethylene (HDPE). The fuel pump and gasoline level sensor are housed in a fuel pump module that is part of the tank.

Fuel pump

Fuel is drawn out of the tank and delivered to the engine via the fuel pump. It guarantees a constant fuel flow at the ideal pressure for combustion. Depending on the architecture of the vehicle, fuel pumps may be mechanical or electronic.

Fuel filter

In between the gasoline tank and the fuel injectors is where you'll find the fuel filter. Its main job is to filter out pollutants and impurities from the gasoline before it gets to the engine. To keep the fuel flowing properly and avoid clogging, fuel filters must be replaced on a regular basis.

Fuel injectors

Precision-engineered parts known as fuel injectors atomize fuel before delivering it right to the engine's combustion chamber. They are in charge of supplying the correct quantity of fuel required for effective combustion. Fuel injectors may accumulate deposits over time, reducing performance and fuel economy.

Fuel lines

To ensure a constant flow of gasoline, fuel lines convey fuel from the fuel tank to the engine. The most common materials used to construct them are strong ones like steel or rubber hoses with high pressure.

Throttle body

The throttle body controls how much air enters the engine, hence regulating the engine's output of power and speed. The fuel injectors, which spray fuel into the intake manifold in conventional fuel systems, are also housed in the throttle body.

Regular Fuel System Maintenance Practices

To keep your traditional fuel system in optimal condition, it is crucial to follow regular maintenance practices. These procedures assist keep problems from occurring and guarantee the durability and effectiveness of your fuel system. Let's examine the major upkeep techniques:

Fuel injector cleaning

Fuel spray patterns and engine performance can be impacted by fuel injector buildup and clogging over time. These deposits can be removed from fuel injectors on a regular basis with the aid of specialized cleaning solutions, restoring normal fuel delivery.

Throttle body cleaning

Additionally, carbon buildup in the throttle body might impact fuel and air delivery. The best fuel-air mixture is achieved with routine throttle body cleaning, which also provides a smooth operation.

Fuel filter replacements

To guarantee continuous fuel flow and stop impurities from entering the engine, fuel filters should be changed at the suggested intervals. The owner's manual for your car should be consulted for precise replacement schedules.

Fuel system inspections

Regular inspections of the fuel system, including fuel lines and connections, can help identify potential leaks or damage. To stop more damage and guarantee proper fuel system operation, it is crucial to fix any problems as soon as possible.

Fuel tank cleaning

Regular fuel tank cleaning helps get rid of silt and other contaminants that may build up over time. This procedure guarantees the fuel's cleanliness and avoids fuel system component fouling.

Fuel quality checks

For your fuel system to operate at its best, it's essential to check the quality of the fuel you use. Fuel that contains water, silt, or other contaminants can harm the parts of the fuel system. Keep a close eye on the fuel you buy to be sure it fulfills specified requirements.

Effects of Traditional Fuel Cars on the Environment and Health

Even though conventional fuel vehicles have long been a dependable form of transportation, it is important to recognize their negative effects on the environment and public health. Let's examine a few crucial elements:

Carbon dioxide emissions

Traditional fuel-powered vehicles add to carbon dioxide (CO_2) emissions, a major contributor to climate change. Fossil fuel combustion puts CO_2 into the atmosphere, which traps heat and causes global warming.

Particulate matter production

Traditional fuels that are burned also release particulate matter into the air, including fine particles and black carbon. The air quality and human health, especially respiratory health, may be negatively impacted by these particles.

Environmental impact of fuel consumption

The extraction, refining, and transportation of traditional fuels have environmental consequences, including habitat destruction, water pollution, and oil spills. Both ecosystems and biodiversity may be harmed by these effects.

Health implications of vehicle emissions

Human health may suffer as a result of exposure to automobile emissions such carbon monoxide (CO), volatile organic compounds (VOCs), and nitrogen oxides (NOx). These pollutants aggravate cardiovascular illnesses, respiratory conditions, and other health concerns.

Alternative Fuel Options

Investigating alternative fuel choices is crucial for a sustainable future given the environmental issues with existing fuel cars. As one of the practical substitutes, compressed natural gas (CNG) will be highlighted in a brief introduction to alternative fuels.

Introduction to alternative fuels

Alternative fuels are non-traditional fuel sources that have fewer emissions and a smaller negative environmental impact than traditional fuels derived from petroleum. They might be produced using renewable resources or offer cleaner combustion.

Overview of compressed natural gas (CNG) as an alternative fuel

A viable alternative fuel for cars is compressed natural gas (CNG). It contains primarily methane gas and is kept under high pressure. When compared to gasoline or diesel, CNG emits fewer pollutants, which helps to enhance the air's quality and lower greenhouse gas emissions. Many vehicles have CNG-compatible systems already installed in them or may be converted to use CNG.

For optimum vehicle performance, fuel economy, and cost savings, the conventional gasoline system must be maintained properly. In order to ensure smooth operation and avoid expensive repairs, routine fuel system maintenance procedures, such as fuel injector cleaning, throttle body cleaning, fuel filter replacements, and fuel system inspections, are necessary. Additionally, investigating alternative fuel options like compressed natural gas (CNG) is a step toward a greener future, especially in light of the environmental impact of standard fuel cars. We can contribute to a more sustainable and effective transportation landscape by prioritizing fuel system maintenance and taking alternative fuels into account.

Chapter 10:

Understanding How Diesel Engines Work

In terms of automotive engines, diesel engines are essential for a variety of vehicles, including trucks, buses, industrial equipment, and power generators. Both amateurs and experts in the automotive industry need to understand how diesel engines operate. The complexities of diesel engines, their advantages over gasoline engines, the parts that make them work, and their uses in diverse industries will all be discussed in this chapter.

What is a Diesel Engine?

An example of an internal combustion engine that burns diesel fuel in its cylinders is a diesel engine. In contrast to gasoline engines, diesel engines use compression ignition, in which the hot air inside the cylinders ignites the fuel on its own. Diesel engines are more efficient than their gasoline equivalents and offer superior fuel economy because the combustion process does not require a spark plug. Diesel engines, however, often operate less well at high speeds than gasoline engines.

How Diesel Engines Differ from Gasoline Engines

Fuel Delivery System

Their fuel distribution systems are one of the main distinctions between diesel and gasoline engines. Diesel engines use fuel injection, in which high-pressure fuel is pumped directly into the combustion chambers. This process ensures effective combustion and improved control over fuel delivery. Contrarily, fuel injectors, which spray fuel into the intake manifold in modern engines, are typically used in gasoline engines.

Fuel Injector Nozzles and Their Role

In diesel engines, fuel injector nozzles are essential. These nozzles are in charge of dispensing a precise fuel spray into the combustion chambers. They guarantee that fuel is distributed and atomized properly, ensuring effective combustion and maximum power output. Engine performance and emissions are greatly impacted by the shape and layout of fuel injector nozzles.

Combustion Process

Diesel engines have a different combustion process than do gasoline ones. Diesel engines use compression ignition, where the high temperature created by the compressed air causes the fuel to ignite on its own. The air-fuel mixture in gasoline engines is ignited by a spark plug, in contrast. The distinctive qualities of diesel engines are a result of this basic distinction in ignition techniques.

High Compression Ratio in Diesel Engines

Diesel engines feature compression ratios that are substantially higher than those of gasoline engines. This indicates that before combustion takes place, the air-fuel mixture in the cylinders is compressed to a significantly smaller volume. With a more effective combustion process and more energy extraction from the fuel, the high compression ratio raises the temperature and pressure inside the cylinders.

Efficiency and Power Output Comparison

Diesel engines outperform gasoline engines in terms of efficiency and power output. Diesel engines' higher compression ratios improve thermal efficiency, which reduces fuel consumption and increases mileage. Additionally, diesel engines provide more torque, which makes them suitable for tasks requiring strong pulling power, such as towing and hauling hefty goods.

Four-Stroke Diesel Engines

The four-stroke cycle, usually referred to as the Otto cycle, is used by the majority of diesel engines. The induction, compression, power, and exhaust strokes are the four steps of this cycle. To properly comprehend how a diesel engine works, it is imperative to comprehend each stage.

Overview of the Four-Stroke Cycle

Beginning with the induction stroke, the four-stroke cycle draws air into the combustion chamber through the inlet valve as the piston descends. For the future steps, this procedure makes sure that the cylinder is filled with new air. The compression stroke comes after the induction stroke, when the piston swings upward and compresses the air inside the cylinder.

Air Intake and the Role of the Inlet Valve

The inlet valve opens during the induction stroke, letting fresh air into the cylinder. Controlling the timing and volume of air intake, maintaining optimal combustion, and enhancing engine performance are all important functions of the inlet valve.

Compression Stroke

Compression of Air and Fuel Preparation

The air that is confined in the cylinder is compressed as the piston rises during the compression stroke. By increasing the temperature and pressure inside the cylinder, this compression gets the air ready for combustion. During this phase, fuel is also fed into the combustion chamber, mixing with the compressed air in advance of ignition.

Power Stroke

Ignition and Combustion Process

The actual combustion and energy creation take place during the power stroke. The injected fuel ignites spontaneously as a result of the high temperature and pressure once the air and fuel mixture inside the cylinder is sufficiently compressed. Gases are rapidly expanded during this combustion process, which forces the piston downward and transforms the energy of combustion into mechanical power.

Role of Fuel Injection Timing and Pressure

Diesel engine combustion is substantially impacted by the time and pressure of fuel injection. The timing and pressure are precisely controlled to provide optimal combustion, effective energy extraction, and minimal emissions. In order to maximize performance and fuel efficiency, modern diesel engines use sophisticated fuel injection systems that can change the timing and pressure in response to different operating situations.

Exhaust Stroke

Expulsion of Burned Gases

During the exhaust stroke, the piston moves upward, expelling the burned gases produced during the power stroke. As soon as the exhaust valve opens, the gases can flow out of the cylinder and into the exhaust system. Effective exhaust gas removal is essential for preserving engine performance and reducing emissions.

Operation of the Exhaust Valve

The timing and length of gas expulsion are controlled by the exhaust valve, which is essential in the exhaust stroke. During the second induction stroke, it permits new air to enter and guarantees that the gases escape the cylinder smoothly.

Diesel engines efficiently transform the energy released during fuel combustion into meaningful mechanical effort by using the four-stroke cycle. Through this procedure, diesel engines are guaranteed to give the strength, effectiveness, and dependability needed for a variety of applications in the automotive, industrial, and power generation industries. Having a thorough understanding of the four-stroke cycle can help you better understand how diesel engines work and how important each stage is to the engine's overall performance.

Chapter 11:

Hybrid Vehicles

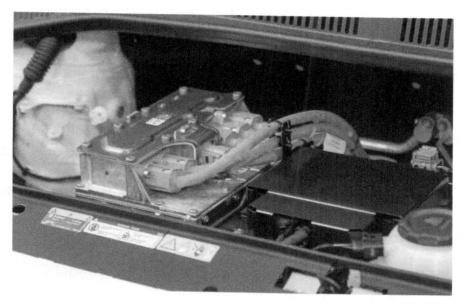

The world of automobile technology is developing quickly, and hybrid cars have gained popularity recently. These hybrid vehicles, which provide a number of advantages like increased fuel efficiency and lower emissions, combine an internal combustion engine with an electric motor. To guarantee optimal performance and longevity, hybrids need routine maintenance and repair, just like any other type of vehicle.

Understanding Hybrid Vehicles

The power of an internal combustion engine and an electric motor are combined in hybrid vehicles according to a novel operating theory. Together, they enable increased fuel economy and less environmental effect. There are several varieties of hybrid vehicles, each with a unique operating concept and set of benefits, including series hybrids, parallel hybrids, and series-parallel hybrids.

Common Components in Hybrid Vehicles

We must become familiar with the main parts of hybrid vehicles in order to comprehend maintenance and repair. They are the internal combustion engine, regenerative braking system, transmission system, battery pack, electric motor, and power control unit (PCU). Every part of a hybrid vehicle is essential to its overall operation.

Benefits of Hybrid Vehicles

Comparing hybrid automobiles to standard gasoline-powered cars, there are various benefits. They first benefit the environment by lowering greenhouse gas emissions and reliance on fossil fuels. Hybrid vehicles also provide greater fuel economy and cost savings, enabling drivers to reduce their fuel costs. Hybrid vehicles are further made enticing by the frequent availability of tax breaks and refunds for their owners.

Maintenance Tips for Hybrid Vehicles

For hybrid vehicles to run smoothly and last a long time, regular maintenance is necessary. Following a suggested inspection and maintenance schedule, which includes inspecting the cooling system, electrical system, battery, engine, brakes, tires, and tires, is one maintenance recommendation. Hybrid vehicle maintenance is essential in all areas, including battery care and replacement, engine oil changes, brake system care, tire rotation, and cooling system care.

Typical Problems with Hybrid Vehicles Despite their generally high level of dependability, hybrid cars occasionally have faults that need to be fixed. Deterioration and eventual replacement of batteries are common battery-related issues. Problems with the vehicle's converter and inverter can also occur, reducing its overall performance. Other potential problems that owners of hybrid vehicles can have include issues with the engine's emissions and performance, brake system issues, transmission issues, and electrical system failures.

Choosing a Hybrid Vehicle Repair Shop

It's critical to locate a trustworthy and skilled repair facility when needing hybrids repaired. Hybrid technology-savvy certified technicians are a requirement. When choosing a hybrid vehicle repair facility, it's important to take into account things like reliable diagnostic equipment, satisfied clientele, and warranty coverage.

Diagnosing Hybrid Vehicle Problems

Understanding hybrid-specific error codes and warning lights is necessary for problem-solving with these vehicles. For proper diagnostics, specialist equipment and software may be needed for hybrid systems as opposed to conventional automobiles.

Repairing Hybrid Vehicle Components

Repairs for hybrid vehicles include a number of parts. Battery maintenance and repair can assist improve battery performance and life. Repairing converters and inverters is crucial for preserving maximum electrical performance. Hybrid car maintenance and repair includes work on the electrical system, the transmission, the engine, the brake system, and the transmission fluid.

Upgrading Hybrid Vehicles

Owners of hybrid automobiles could think about modifying their cars for better performance and efficiency. The driving experience can be improved, maximizing the advantages of hybrid technology, by upgrading performance, battery capacity, and charging infrastructure.

Hybrid Vehicle Safety Considerations

Specific safety precautions must be followed when working on hybrid automobiles. Hybrid vehicles have high-voltage systems, thus mechanics need to be properly trained to assure their safety. It's imperative to follow safety measures when working on hybrid vehicles, such as shutdown and startup procedures and the wearing of personal protection equipment.

Future of Hybrid Vehicles

Hybrid vehicles have a bright future as technology develops further. Vehicles that are considerably more efficient and environmentally beneficial will probably be produced as hybrid technology develops. The relevance of hybrid vehicles in influencing the automotive industry is further highlighted by the possibility for further adoption and integration of renewable energy sources.

Hybrid vehicles need regular maintenance and repairs in order to operate at their best and last as long as possible. Hybrid vehicle owners may assure a smooth and joyful driving experience while limiting their environmental impact by being aware of the special parts and systems in hybrid cars, selecting a reputable repair facility, and adhering to suggested maintenance procedures. Hybrid vehicles have enormous potential in the future, and their ongoing development will help make the automobile industry more environmentally friendly and sustainable.

Chapter 12:

Steering and Suspension System

The steering and suspension system is crucial for maintaining a vehicle's performance and making sure the ride is safe and comfortable. The suspension system connects the car to its wheels, providing a pleasant ride by absorbing bumps and keeping the wheels grounded for traction. The steering system enables the driver to direct the vehicle. We will examine the numerous facets of the steering and suspension system in this article, including its parts, types, typical problems, diagnostic techniques, fixes, DIY maintenance advice, and the advantages of using a professional auto repair shop.

Overview of the Steering and Suspension System

Together, the steering and suspension systems improve the driving experience. By reducing the effect of road irregularities and preserving traction, the suspension system ensures a comfortable ride. This is made possible by a system of springs and shock absorbers that dampen and absorb the vertical energy created when the wheels hit bumps. However, the steering system allows for safe maneuverability by allowing the driver to control the direction of the car and making sure the wheels turn when needed.

Importance of Maintaining a Well-Functioning System For a number of reasons, keeping the steering and suspension system in good working order is essential. First of all, it improves driving pleasure by reducing jolts and vibrations experienced within the car, resulting in a comfortable and enjoyable ride. Second, it improves vehicle control and stability, allowing for precise steering and maneuvering. Finally, by ensuring appropriate tire contact with the pavement, enabling effective braking, and lowering the possibility of accidents, a well maintained system adds to overall safety.

Common Signs of Steering and Suspension Issues

Early detection of potential steering and suspension issues can stop additional harm and guarantee the security of the vehicle and its occupants. The steering wheel may be difficult to turn, shake or vibrate, or the steering wheel may not return to its center position after turning. These are some typical symptoms of steering problems. On the other hand, severe bouncing or vibrations, uneven tire wear, tugging to one side of the car, and noisy suspension parts are all typical symptoms of suspension problems. Being aware of these indicators might trigger rapid inspections and essential repairs.

Benefits of Regular Inspections and Maintenance

The steering and suspension system can benefit from routine inspections and maintenance in a number of ways. It assists in averting more serious and expensive repairs later on by proactively recognizing and treating any faults. The safety, comfort, and performance are all maximized. Regular maintenance also improves fuel efficiency, preserves the overall value of the vehicle, and helps components last longer. It is therefore very advantageous to plan inspections as advised by the vehicle's manufacturer or a skilled mechanic.

Steering System

The steering system is made up of a number of parts that cooperate to enable controlled steering and maneuvering.

Components of the Steering System

1. Steering Wheel and Column: The principal point of contact between the driver and the steering system is the steering wheel. It is attached to the steering

column, which connects the rest of the steering system's parts to the driver's input.

2. Steering Gearbox: The steering gearbox transforms the steering wheel's rotating motion into the lateral movement required to spin the wheels.

3. Tie Rods and Tie Rod Ends: The steering gearbox is connected to the wheel spindles by tie rods and tie rod ends, which transfer steering motion and enable wheel alignment modifications.

4. Pitman Arm and Idler Arm: These parts support the steering linkage and transform the steering gearbox's rotating action into lateral movement to regulate the steering angle of the wheels.

Types of Steering Systems

1. Rack and Pinion Steering: In order to translate the steering wheel's rotational motion into lateral movement, this kind of steering system makes use of a rack and pinion mechanism.

2. Recirculating Ball Steering: Recirculating ball steering makes use of a worm gear and ball bearing steering system.

3. Worm and Sector Steering: Worm and sector steering, which is frequently seen in older cars, transmits steering motion using both a worm gear and a sector gear.

Steering Linkages and Geometry

1. Ackermann Steering Geometry: Due to the steering geometry, turns can be made more smoothly by ensuring that the inner front wheel turns at a sharper angle than the outer wheel when cornering.

2. Bell-Crank Steering: Bell cranks and connecting rods are used in bell-crank steering devices to convey steering motion to the wheels.

3. Short Rack-and-Pinion Steering: In order to improve steering response and precision, short rack-and-pinion steering systems use a shorter rack length.

Power Steering

Power steering systems enable drivers to turn the steering wheel with less effort. Power steering systems come in a variety of forms:

1. Hydraulic Power Steering: Systems with hydraulic power steering use hydraulic pressure to assist steering, requiring the driver to do less physical effort.
2. Electric Power Steering: Electric power steering systems offer greater fuel efficiency and control flexibility by using an electric motor to provide steering assistance.
3. Electro-Hydraulic Power Steering: In order to give steering assistance while retaining fuel efficiency, electro-hydraulic power steering systems integrate hydraulic and electric technologies.

Suspension System

The suspension system is in charge of minimizing tire-road contact resistance, assuring steering stability, and making sure the ride is comfortable.

Components of the Suspension System

1. Control Arms and Bushings: The suspension system is attached to the car's frame by control arms, also referred to as A-arms. They have bushings, which make movement possible and cushion shocks.
2. Shock Absorbers and Struts: In order to provide ride comfort and stability, shock absorbers and struts moderate the oscillations and vibrations caused by uneven road conditions.
3. Springs: The support and impact absorption functions of coil springs and leaf springs keep the vehicle at a constant height while enabling the suspension to adjust to changing loads and driving conditions.
4. Sway Bar (Stabilizer Bar): Through its connection to the suspension parts on each side of the car, the sway bar reduces body roll when the vehicle is turning.

Types of Suspension Systems

1. Independent Suspension: Better Road contact, handling, and ride quality are all made possible by independent suspension, which enables each wheel to move vertically independently.
2. Dependent Suspension: When bumps or defects are present, dependent suspension systems link the wheels on the same axle, forcing both wheels to move together.

3. MacPherson Strut Suspension: The MacPherson strut suspension streamlines the suspension design and makes space savings by combining the functions of a shock absorber and a suspension arm.
4. Double Wishbone Suspension: The use of two wishbone-shaped control arms on each wheel in a double wishbone suspension allows for fine control of wheel movement and handling.

Suspension Geometry and Alignment

1. Camber, Caster, and Toe: The angle of the wheel with respect to the vertical axis is referred to as camber. Caster is the term denoting the steering axis' forward or backward tilt, which affects the stability of the steering. When viewed from above, the toe describes the angle at which the wheels point inward or outward. For optimum tire wear and vehicle stability, it's critical that these angles are properly aligned.
2. Importance of Proper Alignment: Balanced tire wear, stability, and handling are assured by proper suspension geometry and alignment. Uneven tire wear, reduced fuel efficiency, and poor safety can all result from improper alignment.

Air Suspension

1. Functioning and Benefits: In air suspension systems, air-filled bags take the place of conventional coil or leaf springs. By altering the air pressure in the bags, they provide changeable ride height, increased comfort, and improved handling.
2. Common Issues and Maintenance: Air leaks, broken compressors, and sensor malfunctions are just a few problems that air suspension systems may have. To maintain optimal operation and spot any issues early on, routine maintenance and inspections are required.

Signs of Steering and Suspension Problems

In order to repair steering and suspension problems quickly and stop future damage, it is crucial to understand their symptoms.

Steering Issues

1. Difficulty Turning the Steering Wheel: The steering system may be experiencing issues, such as worn out parts or low power steering fluid, if it is stiff or unresponsive.
2. Steering Wheel Vibration or Shaking: The steering wheel shaking or vibrating could indicate damaged or out-of-balance parts.
3. Steering Wheel Not Returning to Center: When turning, if the steering wheel does not automatically return to the center position, there may be a problem with the steering linkage or alignment.

Suspension Issues

1. Excessive Bouncing or Vibrations: Driving with excessive bouncing or vibrations may indicate worn shocks or struts.
2. Uneven Tire Wear: Uneven tire wear across the tread area may be a sign of worn or misaligned suspension parts.
3. Vehicle Pulling to One Side: Driving-related drifting or pulling to one side may be a sign of alignment or suspension issues.
4. Noisy Suspension Components: Unusual noises while driving over bumps, such as clunking, squeaking, or knocking sounds, may be a sign of worn or damaged suspension parts.

Diagnosing Steering and Suspension Problems

For successful repairs and maintenance, steering and suspension issues must be accurately diagnosed.

Visual Inspection: Visually examine the steering and suspension parts carefully for any indications of wear, damage, or fluid leaks.

Road Test and Performance Evaluation: To assess the vehicle's steering responsiveness, stability, and ride comfort, test it on several types of road surfaces.

Suspension System Measurements and Testing: Measure suspension angles, evaluate ride height, and spot anomalies using specialist equipment.

Using Diagnostic Tools and Equipment: For a thorough evaluation, use diagnostic tools, such as computerized systems, to collect fault codes and evaluate sensor data.

Common Steering and Suspension Repairs

A number of typical fixes take care of steering and suspension problems and guarantee the system is operating correctly.

Tie Rod End Replacement: Tie rod ends that are worn out or damaged may cause steering play or misalignment and need to be replaced.

Control Arm Bushing Replacement: Control arm bushings that are worn out or degraded can produce noise, vibrations, and poor handling, which calls for replacement.

Shock Absorber or Strut Replacement: To regain ride comfort and stability, damaged or worn-out shock absorbers or struts should be replaced.

Coil Spring Replacement: To keep the suspension working properly and the ride height at the right level, broken or sagging coil springs should be changed.

Sway Bar Link Replacement: Sway bar links that are worn out or damaged may cause the vehicle to roll more and be less stable, necessitating repair.

Wheel Alignment: Toe, caster, and camber angles should be adjusted during wheel alignment to provide optimal tire wear and stability.

DIY Maintenance Tips

While some steering and suspension repairs need for specialized knowledge, there are upkeep procedures that car owners may complete on their own to keep the system in good working order.

Regular Inspection: Visually inspect the steering and suspension parts for signs of deterioration, leaks, or damage.

Keep Components Clean: Clean the parts frequently to get rid of debris, grime, and salt from the road that could hasten wear and corrosion.

Check Tire Pressure: To achieve consistent tire wear and ideal handling, keep the recommended tire pressure.

Lubricate Components: To reduce friction and stop early wear, properly lubricate steering and suspension parts including ball joints and bushings.

Follow Manufacturer's Maintenance Schedule: Follow the suggested maintenance schedule provided by the vehicle's manufacturer for regular inspections, fluid changes, and part replacements.

Professional Auto Repair Services

DIY maintenance is advantageous, but some steering and suspension repairs call for trained professionals and specific tools.

Choosing a Reliable Auto Repair Shop: Choose a steering and suspension repair specialist from a trustworthy, licensed auto repair shop.

Qualified Technicians: Make sure the repair facility hires certified specialists with knowledge of steering and suspension systems.

Use of Quality Parts: Make sure the repair facility only employs high-quality replacement parts to guarantee longevity and effectiveness.

Comprehensive Inspections and Diagnostic Tools: Professional vehicle repair companies are equipped with the tools needed to conduct in-depth analyses, identify intricate problems, and make precise repairs.

Warranty and Guarantees: Ask the repair company what assurances and warranties they offer on the parts and labor they install.

A safe, comfortable, and enjoyable driving experience depends on the steering and suspension system. To ensure the highest level of performance, stability, and safety, regular inspections, maintenance, and prompt repairs are essential. Although car owners can conduct some maintenance activities themselves, it is best to use professional auto repair services for complicated fixes and diagnostics. You can extend the life of your car and guarantee a comfortable ride by maintaining the steering and suspension system.

Chapter 13:

Tyres, Alignment, and Balance

In order to guarantee a safe and comfortable driving experience, proper wheel alignment and tire maintenance are essential. Neglecting these factors can result in a number of problems, such as shortened tire life, decreased vehicle stability, and poor fuel efficiency. The importance of tyre balancing and alignment will be discussed in detail in this article, along with how they affect tire performance, vehicle handling, and overall driving comfort.

Understanding Tyre Alignment

The term "tyre alignment" describes the process of adjusting the angles of the wheels to match the requirements established by the vehicle's manufacturer. As misalignment can greatly alter the tyre's interaction with the road surface, it is intimately tied to the suspension system. Uneven tyre wear, poor vehicle handling, and more strain on the suspension parts can all be consequences of improper alignment.

Camber, toe, and caster are three angles that are changed during tyre alignment. When viewed from the front, the term "camber" describes the vertical tilt of the wheel;

"toe" describes the angle at which the wheels point upward or downward; and "caster" describes the angle of the steering axis when viewed from the side. To guarantee optimum tire performance and vehicle stability, these angles must be properly adjusted.

Signs of Misaligned Tyres

For prompt action and the mitigation of further harm, it is essential to identify the symptoms of misaligned tires. Uneven tread wear is one of the main signs. It indicates misalignment if the tread degrades more quickly on one side of the tire than the other. Additionally, if your car pulls to the left or right without any steering wheel input, your tires are probably out of alignment.

Driving straight and seeing an off-center steering wheel is another warning indication. Misalignment is evident if the steering wheel is not parallel to the trajectory of the car. In addition, tyre imbalance, which can be caused by misalignment, can cause steering wheel vibration. You may treat alignment difficulties quickly and prevent subsequent complications by being aware of these indicators.

Benefits of Tyre Alignment

Investing in routine tire alignment has a number of advantages that make driving safer and more comfortable. The tyres' longer lifespan is a noteworthy benefit. You may extend the life of your tires and prevent early replacements by maintaining even tread wear through appropriate alignment.

Tyre alignment also improves the handling and stability of a vehicle. The vehicle maintains its planned trajectory when the wheels are appropriately aligned, improving control and maneuverability. This is especially important when driving in emergency situations or on rough terrain.

Tyre alignment also eliminates vibration and tugging problems. The steering wheel may vibrate as a result of misaligned tires, which can be uncomfortable and exhausting on lengthy trips. Additionally, good alignment gets rid of the car's propensity to pull to one side, making driving smoother and more predictable.

Finally, improved fuel efficiency is a result of proper tire alignment. Correct wheel alignment results in less rolling resistance, which leads to better fuel efficiency. You can save money on fuel costs and lessen your carbon footprint by frequently having your tires aligned.

Tyre Balancing

Another important component of tyre care is tire balancing. It entails balancing the wheel and tire assembly's weight distribution. Vibrations that can be felt in the steering wheel or throughout the entire vehicle can result from even slight imbalances. These imbalances may result from uneven weight distribution brought on by manufacturing variances or elements like uneven curb wear, loss of balancing weights, or uneven tyre wear.

Unbalanced tires have a substantial impact on vehicle performance and tyre wear. Uncomfortable vibrations from unbalanced tires might be felt by the driver and other passengers. Furthermore, these vibrations have the ability to speed up tire wear and harm suspension parts. You can assure a smoother ride, lessen wear and tear on your tyres, and increase their lifespan by regularly balancing your tires to correct tyre imbalance.

Frequency of Tyre Balancing and Alignment

Tyre balancing should be done on a frequent basis in order to ensure optimal tire performance. The frequency of balancing is influenced by a number of variables, including road conditions, tyre wear patterns, and the effectiveness of earlier balance. Every 5,000 to 6,000 miles or anytime you feel vibrations, it is generally advised to get your tires balanced.

The suggested maintenance intervals for tyre alignment can change based on the car and the road conditions. The best alignment schedule can be found by consulting your car's owner manual or asking a qualified mechanic for advice. Furthermore, certain circumstances, such as running into potholes, curbs, or other road hazards, may necessitate quick alignment checks to stop further harm.

Professional Tyre Alignment Services

To ensure exact and reliable outcomes, it is essential to seek professional assistance with tire alignment. Reputable service providers have a focus on tyre alignment and use sophisticated alignment equipment like Hunter and Hawkeye, which provide a high degree of precision and accuracy. The various alignment angles are measured and adjusted by these systems using cutting-edge technology, guaranteeing that your vehicle's wheels are correctly aligned for optimum performance and safety.

It is crucial to take into account a service provider's experience and standing within the sector when making your choice. Seek out well-known businesses with a history of offering excellent alignment services. You can choose wisely by reading customer reviews and asking for suggestions from reliable sources.

DIY Tyre Maintenance Tips

While professional tyre alignment is essential for the best outcomes, you can do some maintenance tasks at home to augment these services. You can spot alignment problems early on by routinely checking your tires for indications of misalignment, such as uneven tread wear. Using DIY equipment like a toe alignment kit, you can make tiny modifications to the toe angle if you observe a minor misalignment.

It's crucial to remember, though, that exact adjustments and long-term advantages still require professional alignment. DIY techniques should only be used as stopgap measures until you can arrange for a qualified alignment service. You may efficiently maintain your tyres' alignment and extend their life by combining routine checks with expert advice.

Pricing and Payment Options

When searching for tyre alignment and balancing services, pricing transparency is crucial. Reputable service providers provide comprehensive quotations prior to the service, so that you are aware of all associated costs. To avoid unpleasant surprises, it is a good idea to ask about any additional fees or costs.

Most service providers accept a variety of payment choices, including cash, NETS, and VISA. To ensure a simple and hassle-free transaction, it is advised to confirm the approved payment options with the service provider before making an appointment.

Choosing the Right Tyres for Alignment

To achieve the best performance and longevity, it is essential to use tires that can be aligned. Think about things like size, load capacity, and tread pattern when buying new tires or replacing worn-out ones. It's critical to select tires that meet the specs and alignment needs of your vehicle.

Additionally, speaking with a tyre professional or service provider can yield insightful advice. They can assist you in choosing tires that suit your driving style, the state of the road, and the requirements of your car. You may optimize the advantages of expert alignment services and guarantee a secure and comfortable driving experience by picking the appropriate tires for alignment.

For a smoother ride, longer tire life, and better vehicle performance, proper tyre maintenance, alignment, and balance are essential. Recognizing the symptoms of misaligned tyres, such as uneven tread wear, vehicle tugging, an off-center steering wheel, and steering wheel vibrations, requires understanding the idea of tyre alignment and its relationship to vehicle suspension.

You can benefit from benefits like increased tyre lifespan, improved vehicle stability, prevention of vibration and tugging concerns, and improved fuel efficiency by correcting misalignment with the help of professional tyre alignment services. By minimizing tyre imbalance, lowering vibrations, and optimizing tyre wear, routine tire balancing supports alignment.

For precise and accurate outcomes, it is essential to seek professional assistance from renowned service providers outfitted with cutting-edge alignment devices. DIY tyre care can aid in spotting little misalignment, but expert alignment is still required for long-term advantages. A good service experience is facilitated by clear pricing, detailed quotations, and a variety of payment alternatives.

The efficiency of alignment services is increased and optimal performance is ensured by selecting the proper tires that are consistent with alignment criteria. Furthermore, utilizing other services provided by alignment experts can address numerous areas of your vehicle's performance in a thorough manner.

In conclusion, frequent maintenance is crucial for greater vehicle performance, a smoother driving, and longer tire life. Tyre alignment and balancing should also be prioritized. You can profit from a balanced, aligned car by adhering to these procedures, which will increase safety and comfort while driving.

Chapter 14:

Dealing with Emergencies

Unexpected car problems can put drivers in uncomfortable and possibly dangerous circumstances. For one's own safety and to limit future damage, it is essential to be ready for these emergencies and know how to handle them. This article will give readers thorough instructions on how to handle various auto emergencies, ensuring that they have the knowledge they need to deal with these difficult circumstances.

The Importance of Preparedness in Auto Emergencies

Being prepared is essential when dealing with car emergencies. Drivers can react more skillfully to unforeseen situations by adopting a proactive mindset and being aware of the risks. Individuals can safeguard their own security, minimize damage to their vehicles, and quicken the resolution process by being prepared.

Understanding Common Types of Auto Emergencies

There are many different types of auto crises, and each one necessitates a particular course of action. Drivers can more effectively foresee potential problems and respond appropriately by being familiar with frequent sorts of auto crises. This information enables people to manage crises effectively, reducing risks and assuring a quick conclusion.

Safety First: Ensuring Personal Safety

In any auto emergency, putting your own safety first is crucial. People can safeguard themselves and lessen the likelihood of more harm by adhering to a set of safety protocols.

Moving out of Harm's Way

It's critical to swiftly get to safety in the event of an auto emergency. How to protect personal safety in such circumstances is outlined in the stages below:

1. Turning off the Engine

In order to prevent any potential dangers brought on by a malfunctioning car, the first step is to turn off the engine.

2. Activating Hazard Lights

To inform other motorists and signal an emergency situation, it is imperative to turn on the hazard lights.

3. Setting up Emergency Triangle

An extra measure of safety is added by setting up an emergency triangle behind the car to alert approaching vehicles to the situation.

Dealing with a Car Fire

To safeguard oneself and others in the tragic case of a car fire, quick decision-making is essential.

1. Immediate Evacuation

When an automobile is on fire, it's critical to get out as soon as possible and move a safe distance from the flames.

2. Calling for Emergency Services

Making a call to emergency services, such as the fire department, is essential to ensuring that trained personnel are sent out right away to deal with the incident.

Contacting Emergency Services

It's crucial to know how to get in touch with the right emergency services during car emergencies so that you can get the help and support you need.

Ambulance and Medical Assistance

It's important to get medical help right away if you get hurt in an auto emergency. The steps listed below explain how to get in touch with the appropriate medical services:

1. Calling for Ambulance in Case of Injuries

It's critical to contact for an ambulance if there are any injuries. To guarantee that medical personnel get at the location quickly, call emergency services.

2. Non-Emergency Ambulance Contact

Non-emergency ambulance services can provide the essential support and direction when immediate medical attention is not needed but aid is still required.

Reporting the Accident to the Police

A crucial first step in recording the incident and facilitating ensuing insurance claims and legal actions is calling the police to report the accident.

1. Importance of Filing a Police Report

An formal record of the accident is provided by filing a police report, and this record is necessary for insurance claims and any prospective legal actions.

2. Contacting the Police: Emergency Number

People should call the emergency police number to report incidents and request assistance in situations requiring an immediate police presence.

3. Contacting Traffic Police

People can get in touch with the traffic police to report incidents and get advice on what to do next in non-emergency situations or cases involving minor accidents.

Chapter 15:

Keep Your Vehicle Clean and Beautiful

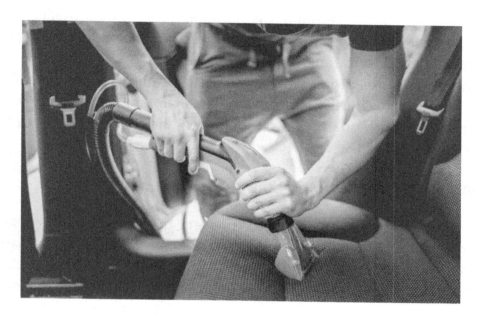

For your car's general health and longevity, it's essential to keep it clean and well-kept. A well-kept car not only improves its aesthetic appeal but also offers a number of performance and financial advantages. We will examine the significance of vehicle upkeep and cleanliness, the advantages of keeping your automobile looking nice, and give an overview of the content plan that will lead us through the numerous facets of auto repair and care in this extensive essay.

Maintenance for Vehicle Longevity

Regular oil changes and fluid checks

1. For the engine of your car to run smoothly and last a long time, engine oil maintenance is essential. To ensure peak performance, the oil filter and engine oil must be checked and changed on a regular basis.
2. Depending on the vehicle and manufacturer's recommendations, different intervals for oil and filter changes are advised. For the engine to remain healthy and function at its best, these intervals must be followed.

Maintaining other vital fluids

1. For safe braking, brake fluid is a crucial component. Brake fluid needs to be regularly checked and replaced to provide optimal braking performance and avoid brake system problems.
2. Coolant, commonly referred to as antifreeze, aids in controlling the engine's temperature. To avoid overheating and engine damage, antifreeze must be regularly checked and replaced.
3. In order to operate automobiles with selective catalytic reduction (SCR) systems, diesel exhaust fluid (DEF) is necessary. To maintain compliance with pollution requirements and guarantee optimum engine performance, DEF must be checked and refilled.

Tire care and maintenance

1. For safe and effective driving, proper tire inflation is essential. The recommended tire pressure should be regularly checked and maintained to increase fuel economy, extend tire life, and enhance vehicle control.
2. Tire rotations on a regular basis help to provide balanced handling, promote even tire wear, and extend tire life. It is crucial to adhere to the manufacturer's suggested tire rotation schedules.
3. It's crucial to be aware of safe tire-changing techniques in case of an emergency. Accidents can be avoided and a safe tire-changing procedure can be achieved by knowing how to operate a jack, remove lug nuts, and replace a tire.

Protecting Your Car's Paint

Understanding paint damage factors

1. If not removed, corrosive chemicals like honeydew and bird droppings can harm the paint. These compounds have acidic ingredients that have the potential to etch through paint and clear coat layers.
2. The paint can also be harmed by insect damage, such as bug splatters. Insect corpses contain acidic substances that, if not immediately cleaned, can cause paint to corrode and become discolored.

Regular car washing and care

1. Based on how often the vehicle is used and the surrounding environment, car wash frequency should be determined. Regular washing aids in removing pollutants, grime, and other buildup from the paint surface.
2. It's crucial to wash the car using clean brushes or rags to prevent harming the paint. Towels made of microfiber and soft car wash gloves are suggested for a secure and efficient cleaning procedure.
3. After cleaning, adding wax gives the paint an additional layer of protection. The surface of the paint is sealed with wax.

Conclusion

To enable readers to confidently navigate the world of automotive maintenance, we have examined numerous facets of maintaining and repairing vehicles in the book "Auto Repair." We have emphasized the significance of routine vehicle maintenance and the early discovery of difficulties throughout the book to stop them from developing into larger problems.

This book's main theme can be summarized as follows: Owners can prevent unexpected car difficulties, secure the long-term dependability and safety of their vehicles, and avoid unanticipated car problems by maintaining a proactive attitude to vehicle care and swiftly attending to concerns.

We have discussed a number of important subjects along the way that every vehicle owner has to be aware of. These subjects cover the value of routine maintenance to keep the car running smoothly, such as oil changes, tire rotations, and fluid checks. We have also dug into more complicated topics, such as diagnosing and fixing typical auto issues, comprehending the many parts of the engine and electrical systems of the car, and advising on when to seek professional assistance.

In order to fulfill our pledge to offer solutions, we have offered the readers useful guidance and doable recommendations. We have equipped readers to do many common maintenance and repair chores on their own, saving them time and money, by providing comprehensive explanations, step-by-step directions, and troubleshooting suggestions. Additionally, we have stressed the significance of locating a trustworthy and respected vehicle repair company when expert assistance is required.

We want readers to take away one major point as we wrap up this book: maintaining your car is important for your safety and the longevity of your investment, as well as for reducing breakdowns. Readers can build a strong foundation of vehicle maintenance knowledge and become proactive stewards of their cars by adhering to the ideas and practices described in this book.

In conclusion, "Auto Repair" aims to give readers a thorough overview of car maintenance, enabling them to take charge of their automotive needs. We aim to have given readers the knowledge and assurance they need to effectively navigate the world of vehicle repair by reiterating the significance of routine maintenance, summarizing the important subjects discussed, and keeping our promise to offer realistic solutions.

Remember, the key to a well-functioning and reliable vehicle lies in your hands. Take the lessons learned from this book and apply them diligently. By doing so, you can ensure a smooth and enjoyable driving experience for years to come.

BONUS:

Car Maintenance: 10 Things Every Car Owner Should Know

The YouTube video titled "Car Maintenance: 10 Things Every Car Owner Should Know - The Short List" provides essential information for car owners to maintain their vehicles properly.

https://www.youtube.com/watch?v=BjX79GsALd8&ab_channel=AutoGuide.com

Here's a brief outline of what you'll learn from the video:

1. Adding Windshield Washer Fluid: You'll learn how to locate and fill the windshield washer fluid reservoir to ensure clear visibility while driving.
2. Replacing Windshield Wipers: The video explains how to replace windshield wipers when they become ineffective, ensuring proper wiping performance and visibility.
3. Checking the Oil: You'll be shown how to check the engine oil level using the dipstick, ensuring it falls within the appropriate range to maintain engine lubrication.

4. Adding Oil: The video demonstrates how to add oil to the engine if the level is low, emphasizing the importance of using the correct viscosity and avoiding overfilling .

5. Checking Tire Pressure: You'll learn the importance of maintaining proper tire pressure for optimal performance and safety, as well as how to use a tire pressure gauge to check and adjust the pressure.

6. Inspecting and Replacing Tires: The video covers the basics of tire inspection, including checking tread depth and identifying signs of wear. It also provides guidance on when and how to replace tires for optimal safety and performance.

7. Changing a Flat Tire: You'll be shown step-by-step instructions on how to safely change a flat tire using a spare tire and the necessary tools.

8. Checking and Replacing Brake Pads: The video explains the importance of maintaining healthy brake pads and demonstrates how to inspect them for wear. It also covers the process of replacing brake pads when necessary.

9. Checking and Topping Up Coolant: You'll learn how to check the coolant level in your car's cooling system and add more if needed to prevent overheating and ensure efficient engine operation.

10. Replacing the Air Filter: The video provides guidance on inspecting and replacing the air filter, which helps maintain clean airflow to the engine for optimal performance and fuel efficiency.

By watching this video, you'll gain valuable knowledge and practical skills to perform these essential car maintenance tasks and keep your vehicle in good shape.

Made in the USA
Middletown, DE
02 October 2023

40006028R00060